# Washington
# NOTARY PRIMER

The NNA's Handbook for Washington Notaries

Fifteenth Edition

Published by:

**National Notary Association**
9350 De Soto Avenue
Chatsworth, CA 91311-4926
Telephone: (800) 876-6827
Fax: (818) 700-0920
Website: NationalNotary.org
Email: nna@NationalNotary.org

©2022 National Notary Association
ALL RIGHTS RESERVED. No part of this book may be reproduced in any form without permission in writing from the publisher.

The information in this *Primer* is correct and current at the time of its publication, although new laws, regulations and rulings may subsequently affect the validity of certain sections. This information is provided to aid comprehension of state Notary Public requirements and should not be construed as legal advice. Please consult an attorney for inquiries relating to legal matters.

Fifteenth Edition, Second Printing ©2022
First Edition ©1986

ISBN: 978-1-59767-301-3

# Table of Contents

Introduction ........................................................................................... 1

Notary Laws Explained ....................................................................... 2

The Notary Commission ..................................................................... 3

Screening the Signer ........................................................................... 7

Checking the Document ................................................................... 14

Notary Acts ......................................................................................... 22

Recordkeeping ................................................................................... 35

Notary Certificate and Stamp .......................................................... 39

In-Person Electronic Notarization and Remote Online
Notarization ....................................................................................... 46

Misconduct, Fines and Penalties ..................................................... 55

Washington Laws Pertaining to Notaries Public .......................... 61

About the NNA ................................................................................... 95

Index .................................................................................................... 96

**Have a Tough Notary Question?**

If you were a National Notary Association member, you could get the answer to that difficult question. Join the NNA® and your membership includes access to the NNA® Hotline* and live Notary experts providing the latest Notary information regarding laws, rules and regulations.

**Hours**
Monday – Friday     5:00 a.m.–6:30 p.m. (PT)
Saturday            5:00 a.m.–5:00 p.m. (PT)

**NNA® Hotline Toll-Free Phone Number: 1-888-876-0827**

After hours you can leave a message or email our experts at Hotline@NationalNotary.org and they will respond the next business day.

*Access to the NNA® Hotline is for National Notary Association members and NNA® Hotline subscribers only. Call and become a member today.

# Introduction

You are to be commended on your interest in Washington Notary law! Purchasing the *Washington Notary Primer* identifies you as a conscientious professional who takes his or her official duties seriously.

In few fields is the expression "more to it than meets the eye" truer than in Notary law. What often appears on the surface to be a simple procedure may have important legal considerations.

The purpose of the *Washington Notary Primer* is to provide you with a resource to help you understand the many complex laws that affect notarization. It takes you through the myriad of Notary laws and puts them in easy-to-understand terms. Every section of the law is analyzed and explained, as well as topics not covered by Washington law but nonetheless of vital concern to you as a Notary.

Whether you are about to be appointed for the first time or are a longtime Notary, we are sure that the *Washington Notary Primer* will provide you with new insight and understanding.

Milton G. Valera
Chairman
National Notary Association

# Notary Laws Explained

This chapter discusses and clarifies key parts of the laws of Washington that regulate Notaries Public. Most of these laws are reprinted in full in "Washington Laws Pertaining to Notaries Public," beginning on page 61.

Most provisions cited are from Chapter 42.45, "Notaries Public," of the Revised Code of Washington (RCW). Other notarial rules are cited from Chapter 308-30, "Notaries Public," of the Washington Administrative Code (WAC).

Additional information about Washington's requirements for Notaries Public is available on the Department of Licensing's website. For step-by-step instructions on the commission application process, applicants may also visit NationalNotary.org. ∎

# The Notary Commission

## Application for Commission

**Qualifications.** To become a Notary in Washington, the applicant must (RCW 42.45.200[1-2]):

- Be at least 18 years old.
- Be a citizen or permanent legal resident of the United States.
- Be a resident or have a place of employment or practice in Washington.
- Be able to read and write the English language.
- Not be disqualified to receive a commission under RCW 42.45.210 (RCW 42.45.200[2]).

**Application.** The applicant must properly complete and submit the Notary application, including the endorsements and personal declaration, and pay the required fees.

**Denial of Application.** The Department of Licensing may deny a Notary application for reasons that include (RCW 42.45.210[1]):

- Unprofessional conduct specified in RCW 18.235.130. (See "Illegal and Improper Acts," pages 58–60.)

- Disciplinary action taken against any professional license in Washington or any other state.

- Engaging in official misconduct as defined under RCW 42.44.160(1) (issuing a false Notary certificate knowing that the contents of the certificate are false), whether or not criminal penalties resulted.

- A violation of any of the provisions of RCW 19.154, relating to immigration services fraud. (See "Immigration Services Fraud Prevention Act," pages 18–20.)

## Notary Bond

**Requirement.** Washington Notaries are required to obtain a $10,000 surety bond.

The bond must be issued by a surety company qualified to issue surety bonds in the state of Washington.

The dates on the bond must coincide exactly with the dates of the Notary's four-year term (RCW 42.45.200[4]).

**Filing the Bond.** The bond must be submitted with the Notary Public application (RCW 42.45.200[4]).

**Purpose.** The Notary bond protects the public from a Notary's misconduct or negligence. The bond does not protect the Notary, who is liable for all damages resulting from illegal or improper performance of notarial duties.

The bond's surety company agrees to pay damages totaling up to the bond amount to persons who suffer financially because of the Notary's improper acts — intentional or not — in the event that the Notary does not have the money to pay these damages. The surety will seek compensation from the Notary for any damages it has to pay out on the Notary's behalf.

**Liable for All Damages.** A Notary and the surety company bonding the Notary may be sued by any person who has been damaged by the Notary's official acts. The surety is liable only up to the amount of the bond, but a Notary may be found liable for any amount of money.

**Errors and Omissions Insurance.** Notaries may choose to purchase insurance to cover any unintentional errors or omissions they may make. Notary errors and omissions insurance provides protection for Notaries who are involved in claims or sued for damages resulting from unintentional notarial errors and omissions. In the event of a claim or civil lawsuit, the insurance company will provide and pay for the Notary's legal counsel and absorb any damages levied by a court or agreed to in a settlement, up to the policy coverage limit. Errors and omissions insurance does not cover the Notary for dishonest, fraudulent or criminal acts or omissions, or for willful or intentional disregard of the law.

## Jurisdiction

**Statewide.** Notaries may perform official acts throughout the state of Washington but not beyond state borders (RCW 42.45.080). Notaries may not witness a signing outside Washington and then return to the state to complete the notarization. All parts of a notarial act must be performed at the same time and place within the state.

## Term of Office

**Four-Year Term.** A Washington Notary Public's term of office is four years, beginning on the effective date specified on the Certificate of Commission and ending at midnight on the commission expiration date (RCW 42.45.200).

## Resignation

**Procedure.** A Notary may resign their commission and/or electronic records and/or remote notary endorsement by notifying the department of this intent in writing (WAC 308-30-270[2]). The Notary seal must be disabled (RCW 42.45.160[1]).

The journal must be kept for 10 years following the date of the last notarization chronicled in the journal (WAC 308-30-270[4]).

## Change of Address

**Procedure.** When a Notary changes his or her address, the Notary must inform the Department of Licensing of the address change

(WAC 308-30-250[1]). The name as shown on the certificate of appointment, along with date of birth, and previous and new addresses, must be included (website, "How to Change Your Name or Address"). Notification may also be made online through Secure-Access Washington or by email.

### Change of Name

**Procedure.** When a Notary changes his or her name, the Notary must notify the Department of Licensing on a form prescribed by the department. A name change notification must be accompanied by a bond rider from the bonding company and a $15 fee for a duplicate Certificate of Commission showing the new name (WAC 308-30-250[1-2]).

**New Seal.** A Notary that submits a name change notification may continue to use their original notary stamp or seal and their original name and signature until they receive a new commission certificate and seal or stamp with the new information (WAC 308-30-250[3]). ∎

# Screening the Signer

## Personal Appearance

**Requirement.** The principal signer must personally appear before the Notary at the time of the notarization (RCW 42.45.040). The Notary and the signer must be face-to-face when the notarization takes place.

For traditional and in-person electronic notarization, this means being in the same physical location as another individual and close enough to see, hear, communicate with, and exchange tangible identification credentials with that individual.

For remote notarial acts, personal appearance means being in a different physical location from another individual but able to see, hear, and communicate with that individual by means of communication technology (WAC 308-30-020).

Notarizations may never be performed over the telephone, nor may they be based on the Notary's recognition of a familiar signature.

## Willingness

**Confirmation.** When performing an acknowledgment, a Notary is stating that the individual has signed a record of the individual's free will for the purpose stated in the record (RCW 42.45.010[1]). The National Notary Association recommends that the Notary confirm that the signer is acting willingly for all notarial acts.

To confirm willingness, the Notary need only ask document signers if they are signing of their own free will. When performing an acknowledgment, the Notary must refuse to notarize if the signer does or says anything that makes the Notary think the signer is being pressured to sign. For other types of notarizations, if the signer does not appear to be signing of his or her own free will, it is recommended that the Notary refuse to proceed.

**Awareness**

**Confirmation.** The Notary should make every effort to confirm that the signer is generally aware of what is taking place.

To confirm awareness, the Notary simply makes a layperson's judgment about the signer's ability to understand what is happening. A document signer who cannot respond intelligibly in a simple conversation with the Notary should not be considered sufficiently aware to sign at that moment. If the notarization is taking place in a medical environment, the signer's doctor can be consulted for a professional opinion. Otherwise, if the signer's awareness is in doubt, the Notary should refuse to notarize.

**Foreign-Language Signers.** Washington law does not prohibit a Notary from notarizing for a signer who does not speak English; however, speaking different languages can make it difficult for a Notary to properly identify the signing party and what is being asked of them. If the Notary has access to a translator that they can rely on, it can help to alleviate this risk (NPG).

**Identifying Document Signers**

**Requirement.** When performing an acknowledgment, a verification on oath or affirmation, and signature witnessing, a Notary must determine, from personal knowledge or satisfactory evidence, that the individual appearing before the Notary has the identity claimed (RCW 42.45.030[1], [2] and [3]).

**Personal Knowledge.** A Notary can identify a signer based on personal knowledge of the identity of the signer (See "Personal Knowledge of Identity", page 9).

**Satisfactory Evidence.** The following two methods of identification are considered to be satisfactory evidence of a signer's identity (RCW 42.45.050[2]):

- Reliable, current identification documents or ID cards (see "Identification Documents," pages 9–10).

- The oath or affirmation of a personally known credible identifying witness who provides satisfactory evidence of his or her identity (see "Credible Identifying Witnesses," pages 10–11).

**Identification for Other Notarial Acts.** While the law does not specify identification standards for certifying a copy, an event, or an act or for protests, the prudent and conscientious Notary will apply the above identification standards to identify all persons requesting a notarial act.

## Personal Knowledge of Identity

**Definition.** The safest and most reliable method of identifying a document signer is for the Notary to depend upon his or her own personal knowledge of the signer's identity. Personal knowledge means familiarity with an individual resulting from interactions with that person over a period of time sufficient to eliminate every reasonable doubt that the person has the identity claimed.

Washington law does not specify how long a Notary must be acquainted with an individual before personal knowledge of identity may be claimed. The Notary's common sense must prevail. In general, the longer the Notary is acquainted with a person, and the more interactions the Notary has had with that person, the more likely the individual is personally known.

## Identification Documents (ID Cards)

**Acceptable Identification Documents.** An identifying document or card relied upon by a Notary to identify a signer must be current, or expired not more than three years before performance of the notarial act. A passport, driver's license, government-issued non-driver identification card, or another form of government identification is acceptable. The identification must contain the signature or a photograph of the individual.

**Multiple Identification.** Identification documents that meet the criteria described above are sufficient to identify a signer. However, a Notary may ask for additional identification, especially if the Notary suspects fraud.

**Name Variations.** The Notary must make sure that the name on the document is the same as the name appearing on the identification presented. In certain circumstances, it may be acceptable for the name on the document to be an abbreviated form of the name on the ID — for example, John D. Smith instead of John David Smith. Last names or surnames, however, should always be the same.

**Fraudulent Identification.** Because phony ID cards are common, the Notary should scrutinize each card for evidence of tampering or counterfeiting, or for evidence that it is a genuine card issued to an impostor.

Some clues that an ID card may have been fraudulently altered include mismatched type styles, a photograph raised from the surface, a signature that does not match the signature on the document, unauthorized lamination of the card and smudges, erasures, smears or discolorations.

### Credible Identifying Witnesses

**Purpose.** When a document signer is not personally known to the Notary and is not able to present reliable ID cards, that signer may be identified on the oath or affirmation of a credible identifying witness (RCW 42.45.050[2]).

**Qualifications.** A credible identifying witness must be personally known to the Notary and the document signer, and must provide satisfactory evidence of his or her identity (RCW 42.45.050[2]).

A reliable credible identifying witness should have a reputation for honesty. The witness should be a capable individual who would not be tricked, bullied or otherwise influenced into identifying someone he or she does not really know. Ideally, the witness should have no personal, beneficial or financial interest in the transaction requiring a notarial act.

**Oath (Affirmation) for Credible Identifying Witness.** An oath or affirmation must be administered to the credible identifying witness by the Notary to compel truthfulness.

If not otherwise prescribed by law, a Washington Notary may use the following or similar wording to administer an oath or affirmation to a credible identifying witness:

> Do you solemnly swear that you personally know this signer truly holds the identity he (or she) claims, so help you God?

> (Do you solemnly affirm that you personally know this signer truly holds the identity he (or she) claims?)

**Journal Entry.** If the Notary keeps a journal, the credible identifying witness's name and residence address should be recorded. Prudent Notaries will also ask the witness to sign the journal in the column where the Notary indicates how the signer was identified.

## Signature by Mark

**Mark Serves as Signature.** A person who cannot sign his or her name because of illiteracy or a physical disability may instead use a mark — an "X," for example — as a signature.

**Witnesses for Notarization.** For a signature by mark to be notarized, there should be two impartial witnesses (in addition to the Notary) to the making of the mark. Both witnesses also should sign the document, and one witness should write out the marker's name beside the mark. It is recommended that a mark also be affixed in the Notary's journal, if kept, and that the witnesses also sign the journal.

**Notarization Procedures.** Because a properly witnessed mark is regarded as a legal signature, no special procedures or certificates are required. The person making the mark must be positively identified, as with any other signer, and regular Notary certificates may be used.

### Signature by Proxy

**Signature if Individual Unable to Sign.** Washington law allows for taking the acknowledgment of a person who is physically unable to sign his or her name or make a mark. In such a situation, the person with the disability may direct an appointee other than the Notary to sign on his or her behalf (RCW 42.44.080[2] and 64.08.100).

**Procedure.** As for any acknowledgment, the Notary must verify that the signer is voluntarily executing the document and must identify the signer through personal knowledge or satisfactory evidence.

In addition, the notarial officer must insert "signature affixed by (name of appointee) at the direction of (name of individual)" or words of similar import (RCW 42.45.070).

**Certificate.** The Notary's acknowledgment certificate must state the Notary's name and place of residence and that the principal's signature was affixed according to RCW 64.08.100.

When no notarial wording is provided, the National Notary Association suggests the following wording:

State of Washington    )
County of _____ )

I certify that I know or have satisfactory evidence that _____ (name of person unable to sign) is the person who appeared before me and that said person was unable to write his/her name or to make a mark and appears otherwise capable, and that said person orally directed me to write his/her signature on this instrument on his/her behalf under authority of RCW 64.08.100, and acknowledged it to be his/her free and voluntary act for the uses and purposes mentioned in the attached instrument.

Dated: _____

_____ (Signature of Notary)    (Seal/Stamp of Notary)

Notary Public — State of Washington

My Commission Expires: _____

**Journal Entry.** The Notary must record the specific circumstances of the notarization in a journal.

## Notarizing for Minors

**Under Age 18.** Generally, persons must reach the age of majority before they can handle their own legal affairs and sign documents for themselves. In Washington, the age of majority is 18. Normally, parents or court-appointed guardians will sign on a minor's behalf. In certain cases, minors may lawfully sign documents and have their signatures notarized — minors engaged in business transactions or children serving as court witnesses, for example.

**Include Age Next to Signature.** When notarizing for a minor, the Notary should ask the young signer to write his or her age next to the signature on the document and in the journal. This will alert any interested party that the signer is a minor. The Notary is not required to verify the minor's age.

**Identification.** The method for identifying a minor is the same as that for an adult. However, determining the identity of a minor can be problematic because minors often do not possess acceptable identification documents, such as driver's licenses or passports. If the minor does not have an acceptable ID, then the other methods of identifying signers must be used: either the Notary's personal knowledge of the minor or the oath or affirmation of a credible identifying witness who can identify the minor. (See "Identifying Document Signers," pages 8–9.) ∎

# Checking the Document

**Blank or Incomplete Documents**

**Blank/Incomplete Documents.** Washington law does not address notarizing blank or incomplete documents. However, any blanks in a document should be filled in by the signer prior to notarization. The Notary may not tell the signer what to write in the blanks. If the signer is unsure what to write, he or she should contact the document's issuer, its eventual recipient, or an attorney.

**Photocopies & Faxes**

**Original Signature.** A photocopy or fax may be notarized as long as the signature on it is original, meaning that the photocopy or fax must have been signed with pen and ink. Signatures on documents presented for notarization must always be signed with a handwritten, original signature. A photocopied or faxed signature may never be notarized.

Public recorders sometimes will not accept notarized photocopies or faxes, because the text of the document may be too faint to adequately reproduce in microfilming.

## Disqualifying Interest

**Impartiality.** Notaries are appointed by the state to be impartial, disinterested witnesses whose screening duties help ensure the integrity of important legal and commercial transactions. Lack of impartiality by a Notary throws doubt on the integrity and lawfulness of any transaction.

Washington Notaries are expressly prohibited from notarizing a document in which they are a signer (RCW 42.45.020). By extension, this means that Notaries may never notarize their own signatures and, in most cases, that they may not notarize documents in which they are named.

**Financial or Beneficial Interest.** A Notary may not perform any notarization related to a transaction in which that Notary has a direct financial or beneficial interest.

A financial or beneficial interest exists when the Notary is individually named as a principal in a financial transaction or when the Notary receives an advantage, right, privilege, property or fee valued in excess of the lawfully prescribed notarial fee.

With regard to real estate transactions, a Notary is generally considered to have a disqualifying financial or beneficial interest when that Notary is a grantor or grantee, mortgagor or mortgagee, trustor or trustee, lessor or lessee, or a beneficiary in any way of the transaction.

**Relatives.** A notarial officer may not perform a notarial act with respect to a record to which the officer or the officer's spouse or domestic partner is a party, or in which any of the above have a direct beneficial interest.

Even if a Notary has no interest in the document and does not attempt to influence the signer, notarizing for a relative could subject the document to a legal challenge if other parties to the transaction allege the Notary could not have acted impartially.

## Refusal of Services

**Discrimination.** Notaries should honor all lawful and reasonable requests to notarize. A person's race, age, gender, religion, nationality, ethnicity, lifestyle or political viewpoint is never legitimate cause for refusing to perform a notarial act.

Noncustomers. An employer may limit the services of Notary-employees to business-related notarizations during hours of employment and exclude services to the general public. Notary-employees may refuse to notarize for noncustomers if their employer has limited their services in this manner.

### Reasonable Care

**Responsibility.** As public servants, Notaries must act responsibly and exercise reasonable care in the performance of their official duties. If a Notary fails to do so, he or she may be subject to a lawsuit to recover financial damages caused by the Notary's error or omission.

In general, reasonable care is that degree of concern and attentiveness that a person of normal intelligence and responsibility would exhibit. If a Notary can show a judge or jury that he or she did everything expected of a reasonable person, the judge or jury is obligated by law to find the Notary not liable for damages.

Complying with all pertinent laws is the first rule of reasonable care for a Notary. If there are no statutory guidelines in a given instance, the Notary should take all reasonable steps to use common sense and prudence.

### Unauthorized Practice of Law

**Do Not Assist with Legal Matters.** A nonattorney Notary may not assist another person in drafting, completing, selecting or understanding a document or transaction requiring a notarial act. A nonattorney Notary may not give legal advice or accept fees for legal advice (RCW 42.45.230[1]).

The Notary should not fill in blank spaces in the text of a document for other persons, tell others what documents they need or how to draft them or advise others about the legal sufficiency of a document — and especially not for a fee.

A Notary, of course, may fill in the blanks on the Notary certificate. And a Notary, as a private individual, may prepare legal documents to which he or she is personally a party, but the Notary may not then notarize his or her signature on those documents.

Notaries who overstep their authority by advising others on legal matters are guilty of a gross misdemeanor for the first offense. Each subsequent offense is a class C felony (RCW 2.48.180[3]).

**Exceptions.** Nonattorney Notaries who are specially trained, certified or licensed in a particular field (e.g., real estate, insurance or escrow) may advise others about documents in that field only. In addition, trained paralegals under the supervision of an attorney may advise others about documents in routine legal matters.

## Authentication

**Documents Sent Out of State.** Documents notarized in Washington and sent out of state may be required to bear proof that the Notary's signature and seal are genuine and that the Notary had authority to act at the time of notarization. This process of proving the genuineness of an official signature and seal is called authentication or legalization.

In Washington, the proof is in the form of an authenticating certificate attached to the notarized document by the Secretary of State's office. For additional information, visit sos.wa.gov/corps/apostilles/.

The original notarized document must be forwarded with a written request, the Notary's name, the Notary's commission expiration date and the fee. It is not the Notary's responsibility to obtain, pick up or pay for the authenticating certificate.

**Documents Sent Out of Country.** If a notarized document will be sent outside the United States, a chain-authentication process may be necessary, and additional authenticating certificates may have to be obtained from the U.S. Department of State and different ministries of a given foreign nation, here and abroad. This chain-certification process can be time-consuming and expensive. Contact the Secretary of State's office at (360) 725-0344 for more information.

**Apostilles and the Hague Convention.** Fortunately, more than 100 nations, including the United States, subscribe to a treaty under the auspices of the Hague Conference that simplifies authentication of notarized documents exchanged between any of these nations.

The official name of this treaty, adopted by the Conference on October 5, 1961, is *The Hague Convention Abolishing the Requirement of Legalization for Foreign Public Documents.*

Under the Hague Convention, only one authenticating certificate called an *apostille* is necessary to ensure acceptance of a Notary's signature and seal in these subscribing countries. (*Apostille* means "notation" in French.) In Washington, *apostilles* are issued by the Secretary of State. The fees and procedures are the same as for obtaining an ordinary authenticating certificate, except that the country for which the document is destined should also be specified in the written request.

### Foreign Languages

**Foreign-Language Documents.** Although Washington Notaries are not expressly prohibited from notarizing documents written in a language they cannot read, there are difficulties and dangers in doing so: The document may be misrepresented to the Notary, a blatant fraud may go undetected, the Notary may inadvertently perform an incorrect or illegal notarial act, and making a complete journal entry may be difficult.

Ideally, a foreign-language document should be referred to a Notary who reads that language. In large cities, such multilingual Notaries are often found in ethnic neighborhoods or in foreign consulates.

If a Notary chooses to notarize a document that he or she cannot read, the notarial certificates must either be in English, or in dual-languages where one of the languages is English (NPG).

### Immigration Services Fraud Prevention Act

**Purpose.** Enacted into law in 2011, the *Immigration Services Fraud*

*Prevention Act* addresses deceiving practices of unscrupulous nonattorney Notaries and other unauthorized persons engaging in the practice of law in an immigration matter for compensation.

**Prohibitions.** A Washington Notary or any person who is not licensed to practice law or who is not permitted to represent others under federal law in an immigration matter may not, for compensation (RCW 19.154.060[2]):

- Advise or assist another person in determining the person's legal or illegal status for the purpose of an immigration matter.

- Select or assist persons in selecting, or advise another as to his or her answers on, a government agency form or document in an immigration matter.

- Select or assist persons in selecting, or advise another in selecting, a benefit, visa, or program to apply for in an immigration matter.

- Solicit to prepare documents for, or represent the interests of, persons in a judicial or administrative proceeding in an immigration matter.

- Explain, advise, or interpret the meaning or intent of a question on a government agency form in an immigration matter.

- Charge a customer a referral fee for referring the individual to an attorney.

- Select, draft, or complete legal documents affecting the legal rights of persons in an immigration matter.

Furthermore, a nonattorney Notary, regardless of whether compensation is sought, may not (RCW 19.154.060[3] and [5]):

- Represent that he or she is a *Notario Publico, Notario,* immigration assistant, immigration consultant or immigration specialist, or use any other designation or title in any language conveying or implying that the Notary possesses legal skills in the areas of immigration law in oral statements or in any document, advertisement, stationery, business card, website or comparable written material.

- Represent that he or she can or is willing to provide services in an immigration matter, if such services would constitute the practice of law. The prohibition extends to making oral statements or to making representations in any document, advertisement, stationery, business card, website or comparable written material.

**Exceptions.** The prohibitions cited above do not apply to the following persons in the following scenarios (RCW 19.154.060[4]):

- Nonlawyer assistants acting under the supervision of a licensed Washington attorney or a person permitted to practice law or represent others under federal law in an immigration matter.

- Persons offering translation services related to words contained on a government form from English to another language and translating a person's words from another language to English, regardless of whether compensation is sought.

In addition, persons not licensed to practice law or represent others under federal law in an immigration matter are not prohibited from offering translation services, regardless of whether compensation is sought. Translating words contained on a government form from English to another language and translating a person's words from another language to English does not constitute the unauthorized practice of law (RCW 19.154.060[4]).

**Penalties.** A violation of the *Immigration Services Fraud Prevention Act* is punishable as an unfair and deceptive practice and method of competition as set forth in RCW 19.86.020 (RCW 19.154.090[1]).

In addition, any person proximately injured by a violation of the Act may bring a civil action to recover actual damages or $1,000, whichever is greater (RCW 19.154.090[2]).

Finally, a violation of any provision of the Act is punishable as a gross misdemeanor, and a violation specifically by a Washington Notary constitutes unprofessional conduct under RCW 18.235 and may be grounds for the Director of Licensing to deny an application for commission as a Notary (RCW 19.154.100 and 44.42.030[1][c]).

## Wills

**Do Not Offer Advice.** People often attempt to draw up wills on their own without benefit of legal counsel and then bring these homemade testaments to a Notary to have them "legalized," expecting the Notary to know how to proceed. In advising or assisting such persons, the Notary risks prosecution for the unauthorized practice of law. The Notary's ill-informed advice might do considerable damage to the affairs of the signer and subject the Notary to a lawsuit to recover losses.

Wills are highly sensitive documents whose format is dictated by strict laws. The slightest deviation from these laws can nullify a will. In some cases, handwritten wills have actually been voided by notarization because the document was not entirely in the handwriting of the testator.

**Do Not Proceed Without Certificate Wording.** A Notary should notarize a will only if a Notary certificate is provided for each signer, and the signers are not asking questions about how to proceed. Any such questions should be answered by an attorney.

**Living Wills.** Documents that are popularly called living wills may be notarized. These are not actually wills at all, but written statements of the signer's wishes concerning medical treatment in the event that the signer has an illness or injury and is unable to issue instructions on his or her own behalf. ■

# Notary Acts

## OFFICIAL NOTARY ACTS

### Authorized Acts

Notaries may perform the following official acts (RCW 42.45.010[8]):

- **Acknowledgments**, a declaration by an individual in the presence of a notarial officer stating that the individual has signed a record of the individual's free will for the purpose stated in the record and, if the record is signed in a representative capacity, the individual also declares that he or she signed the record with proper authority and signed it as the act of the individual or entity identified in the record. (See pages 23–25.)

- **Certified Copies**, certifying that a photocopy of an original document is true and complete. (See pages 25–26.)

- **Depositions**, certifying that the spoken words of a witness were accurately taken down in writing. Although Notaries are authorized to take them, depositions are typically performed by skilled court reporters. (See pages 26–27.)

- **Oaths and Affirmations**, which are solemn promises to a Supreme Being (oaths) or solemn promises on one's own personal honor (affirmations). (See pages 27–28.)

- **Verifications Upon Oath or Affirmation**, a declaration, made by an individual on oath or affirmation before a notarial officer, that a statement in a record is true. (See pages 28–29.)
- **Witnessing Signatures**, certifying that a signer personally appeared before the Notary, was identified by the Notary and signed the document in the Notary's presence. (See pages 29–30.)
- **Certifying an Event or Act**, certifying that an event or act has occurred or has been performed. (See pages 30–31.)
- **Protests**, certifying that a negotiable instrument or other written promise to pay was not honored. (See pages 31–33.)

### Acknowledgments

**Purpose.** Acknowledgments are one of the most common forms of notarization. Typically, they are executed on deeds and other documents affecting real property that will be publicly recorded by a county auditor.

**Procedure.** In executing an acknowledgment, the Notary certifies the following (RCW 42.45.010[1] and 42.44.080[1]):

1. The signer *personally appeared* before the Notary on the date and in the county indicated on the Notary certificate.

2. The signer was *positively identified* by the Notary through personal knowledge or satisfactory evidence. (See "Identifying Document Signers," pages 8–9.)

3. The signer *acknowledged* to the Notary that the signature was freely made for the purposes stated in the document and, if the document is signed in a representative capacity, that he or she had proper authority to do so. (If a document is willingly signed in the presence of the Notary, this act can serve just as well as an oral statement of acknowledgment.)

**Witnessing Signature Not Required.** For an acknowledgment, the document does not have to be signed in the Notary's presence. As long as the signer appears before the Notary at the time of notarization to acknowledge having voluntarily signed the document for the purposes stated in it, the Notary may execute the acknowledgment (RCW 42.45.010[1]).

**Representative Capacity.** An individual may acknowledge the signature on a document as a representative of another person (e.g., as an attorney in fact) or of an impersonal legal entity (e.g., as a corporate officer).

The following representative capacities are recognized by Washington law (RCW 42.45.010[7][a-d]):

- An authorized officer, agent, partner, trustee or other representative on behalf of a corporation, partnership, trust or other entity.

- A public officer, personal representative, guardian or other representative in a capacity specified in the document.

- An attorney in fact for a principal signer.

- An authorized representative of another person in any other capacity.

**Certificates for Acknowledgments.** Washington law provides wording for acknowledgment certificates that accommodate signers in individual and corporate capacities:

- Acknowledgment by Individual (RCW 42.45.140[1]):

    State of Washington  )
    County of _____ )

    This record was acknowledged before me on _____ (date) by _____ (name(s) of individuals).

    _____ (Signature of Notary)   (Stamp of Notary)
    Notary Public — State of Washington
    My Commission Expires: _____

- Acknowledgment in a Representative Capacity (RCW 42.45.140[2]):

    State of Washington    )
    County of _____  )

    This record was acknowledged before me on _____ (date) by _____ (name(s) of individuals) as _____ (type of authority, such as officer or trustee) of _____ (name of party on behalf of whom record was executed).

    _____ (Signature of Notary)     (Stamp of Notary)
    Notary Public — State of Washington
    My Commission Expires: _____

## Certified Copies

**Purpose.** Washington Notaries have authority to certify (or attest) that a copy of an original document is a complete and true reproduction of the document that was copied (RCW 42.45.030[4]).

**Procedure.** The custodian of the document must present the document to the Notary and request a certified copy. Ideally, the Notary should make or supervise the making of the copy. This reduces the risk of fraud.

Regardless of how the copy is made, the Notary must carefully compare the copy to the original, to be sure that the copy is a full, true and accurate reproduction of the original (RCW 42.45.030[4]).

A certified copy does not have to be made from an original document. A photocopy may serve as the original as long as it is so described (e.g., a copy of a University of Washington degree).

**Precautions.** Though certification of a transcription or hand-rendered copy is permitted under Washington law, the National Notary Association strongly recommends that Notaries only certify photocopies in order to avert the likelihood that something may be inadvertently omitted in a handmade copy.

**Excluded Documents.** Notaries should not certify copies of vital or public records or of recordable documents (e.g., birth or death certificates, documents affecting title to real property). A Notary's "certification" of such a copy may lend credibility to what is actually a counterfeit or altered document. Only officials in the appropriate public records office may certify copies of such certificates and documents.

**Certificate for Certified Copy.** Washington statute provides the following short-form certificate wording for certifying a copy of a document (RCW 42.45.140[5]):

State of Washington        )
County of _____ )


I certify that this is a true and correct copy of a document in the possession of _____ (name of person presenting document) as of this date.


Dated: _____

_____ (Signature of Notary)        (Stamp of Notary)

Notary Public — State of Washington

My Commission Expires: _____

## Depositions

**Purpose.** A deposition is a signed transcript of the signer's oral statements taken down for use in a judicial proceeding. The deposition signer is called the deponent.

With a deposition, both sides in a lawsuit or court case have the opportunity to question the deponent. The questions and answers are transcribed into a written statement, then signed and sworn to before an oath-administering official.

Although Washington law permits any Notary to take depositions (RCW 42.45.140[5]), this duty is most often executed by Notaries who are trained and certified shorthand reporters, also known as court reporters.

**Oath (Affirmation) for Deposition.** Washington statutes prescribe the following wording to administer an oath or affirmation to a deponent prior to taking the deposition (RCW 5.28.020 and 5.28.050):

> You do solemnly swear (affirm) that the evidence you shall give in the issue (or matter) now pending between _____ and _____ shall be the truth, the whole truth, and nothing but the truth, so help you God.

If the oath or affirmation is to be administered to a person other than a witness giving testimony, the wording may be (RCW 5.28.020):

> You do solemnly swear (affirm) you will true answers make to such questions as you may be asked.

When the deponent signs the transcribed deposition, he or she must take a second oath or affirmation, verifying that the contents of the deposition are true. (See "Verifications Upon Oath or Affirmation," pages 28–29.)

### Oaths and Affirmations

**Purpose.** An oath is a solemn, spoken pledge to a Supreme Being. An affirmation is a solemn, spoken pledge on one's own personal honor, with no reference to a Supreme Being. Both are usually a promise or pledge of truthfulness or fidelity and have the same legal effect. In taking an oath or affirmation in an official proceeding, a person may be subject to criminal penalties for perjury should he or she fail to be truthful.

An oath or affirmation can be a full-fledged notarial act in its own right, as when administering an oath of office to a public official, or it can be part of the process of notarizing a document.

A person who objects to taking an oath — pledging to a Supreme Being — may instead be given an affirmation, which does not refer to a Supreme Being.

**Wording for Oath (Affirmation).** If law does not dictate otherwise, a Washington Notary may use the following or similar words in administering an oath or affirmation:

- Oath (affirmation) for an affiant signing an affidavit or a deponent signing a deposition:

    Do you solemnly swear that the statements in this document are true to the best of your knowledge and belief, so help you God?

    (Do you solemnly affirm that the statements in this document are true to the best of your knowledge and belief?)

- Oath (affirmation) for a credible identifying witness identifying a document signer:

    Do you solemnly swear that you personally know this signer truly holds the identity he (or she) claims, so help you God?

    (Do you solemnly affirm that you personally know this signer truly holds the identity he [or she] claims?)

**Response Required.** The oath or affirmation wording must be spoken aloud. The person taking the oath or affirmation must answer affirmatively with "I do," "Yes" or the like. A nod, grunt or other nonverbal reply is not a sufficient response.

**Ceremony and Gestures.** During the administration of an oath or affirmation, the person who swears or affirms holds up his or her hand (RCW 5.28.020). Traditionally, the right hand is raised. Notaries generally have discretion to use words they feel will most compellingly appeal to the conscience of the oathtaker or affirmant.

### Verifications Upon Oath or Affirmation

**Purpose.** While the purpose of an acknowledgment is to positively identify the person taking the acknowledgment, the purpose of a verification upon oath or affirmation is to compel truthfulness by appealing to the signer's conscience and fear of criminal penalties for perjury.

**Procedure.** In executing a verification upon oath or affirmation, a Notary certifies the following (RCW 42.44.080[3]):

- The signer *personally appeared* before the Notary on the date and in the county indicated on the Notary certificate.

- The signer was *positively identified* by the Notary through personal knowledge or satisfactory evidence. (See "Identifying Document Signers," pages 8–9.)

- The *signer signed the document* in the Notary's presence.
- The Notary *administered an oath or affirmation* to the signer.

**Oath (Affirmation) for Verification Upon Oath or Affirmation.** If not otherwise prescribed by law, a Washington Notary may use the following or similar wording to administer an oath or affirmation in conjunction with a verification upon oath or affirmation:

> Do you solemnly swear that the statements in this document are true to the best of your knowledge and belief, so help you God?
>
> (Do you solemnly affirm that the statements in this document are true to the best of your knowledge and belief?)

**Certificate for Verification Upon Oath or Affirmation.** Washington law provides the following short-form certificate wording for a verification upon oath or affirmation (RCW 42.45.140[3]):

> State of Washington   )
> County of _____ )
>
> Signed and sworn to (or affirmed) before me on _____ (date) by _____ (name of individuals making statement).
>
> _____ (Signature of Notary)    (Stamp of Notary)
> Notary Public — State of Washington
> My Commission Expires: _____

## Witnessing or Attesting a Signature

**Purpose.** The act of witnessing (or attesting) a signature is similar to a verification upon oath or affirmation, except that it does not require the signer to take an oath or affirmation. It is used when establishing that the signing date is of major importance.

**Procedure.** In witnessing or attesting a signature, the Notary certifies the following (RCW 42.44.080[4]):

- The signer *personally appeared* before the Notary on the date and in the county indicated on the Notary certificate.

- The signer was *positively identified* by the Notary through personal knowledge or satisfactory evidence. (See "Identifying Document Signers," pages 8–9.)
- The *signer signed the document* in the Notary's presence.

**Certificate for Witnessing or Attesting a Signature.** Washington statute provides the following short-form certificate wording for witnessing or attesting a signature (RCW 42.45.140[4]):

> State of Washington     )
> County of _____ )
>
> Signed or attested before me on _____ (date) by _____ (name of individuals).
>
> _____ (Signature of Notary)     (Stamp of Notary)
> Notary Public — State of Washington
> My Commission Expires: _____

## Certification of an Event or Act

**Purpose.** Washington Notaries have the authority to certify that an event has occurred or an act has been performed (RCW 42.45.010[8]).

**Procedure.** The Notary must determine that the event occurred or the act was performed, based either on personal knowledge or on the sworn or affirmed testimony of a credible witness personally known to the Notary (WAC 308-30-110[2]).

**Document Required.** Certification of an event or act should only be used in conjunction with an attached document (in which the event or act is described). Since Notaries should be impartial, they should not certify events or acts involving themselves (e.g., the Notary mailing a check), which would be similar to a Notary notarizing his or her own signature.

**Certificate for Certifying an Event or Act.** Washington statute provides the following short-form certificate wording for certifying an event or act (RCW 42.45.140[6]):

State of Washington )

County of _____ )

I certify that the event described in this document has occurred or been performed.

_____ (Signature of Notary)     (Stamp of Notary)

Notary Public — State of Washington

My Commission Expires: _____

## Protests

**Purpose.** A Notarial officer may make or note a protest of a negotiable instrument only if the notarial officer is licensed to practice law in this state, acting under the authority of an attorney who is licensed to practice law in this or another state, or acting under the authority of a financial institution regulated by this state, another state, or the federal government. In making or noting a protest of a negotiable instrument the notarial officer or licensed attorney shall determine the matters set forth in RCW 62A.3-505(b) and 42.45.030[5].

A protest is a written statement by a Notary or other authorized officer verifying that payment was not received on an instrument such as a bank draft. Failure to pay is called dishonor. Before issuing a certificate of protest, the Notary must present the bank draft or other instrument to the person, firm or institution obliged to pay, a procedure called presentment (RCW 62A.3-501 to 62A.3-503 and 62A.3-505).

**Antiquated Act.** In the 19th century, protests were common notarial acts in the United States, but they are rarely performed today because of the advent of modern electronic communications and resulting changes in our banking and financial systems. Modern Notaries most often encounter protests in the context of international commerce.

**Special Knowledge Required.** Notarial acts of protest are complicated and varied, requiring a special knowledge of financial and legal terminology. Only Notaries who have this special knowledge, or who are acting under the supervision of an experienced bank officer or an attorney familiar with the Uniform Commercial Code, should attempt a protest.

**Certificate for Protest.** Washington law prescribes the following wording for execution of a notice of dishonor. The notice of dishonor must be sent by mail to the drawer of the check at the drawer's last known address. The notice must be in substantially the following form (RCW 62A.3-520):

> NOTICE OF DISHONOR OF CHECK
>
> A check drawn by you and made payable by you to in the amount of has not been accepted for payment by _____, which is the drawee bank designated on your check. This check is dated _____, and it is numbered, No. _____.
>
> You are CAUTIONED that unless you pay the amount of this check within fifteen days after the date this letter is postmarked, you may very well have to pay the following additional amounts:
>
> (1) Costs of collecting the amount of the check, including an attorney's fee which will be set by the court;
>
> (2) Interest on the amount of the check which shall accrue at the rate of twelve percent per annum from the date of dishonor; and
>
> (3) Three hundred dollars or three times the face amount of the check, whichever is less, by award of the court.
>
> You are also CAUTIONED that law enforcement agencies may be provided with a copy of this notice of dishonor and the check drawn by you for the possibility of proceeding with criminal charges if you do not pay the amount of this check within fifteen days after the date this letter is postmarked.
>
> You are advised to make your payment to _____ at the following address: _____.

In addition to sending a notice of dishonor to the drawer of the check, the Notary must execute an affidavit certifying service of the notice by mail. The affidavit of service by mail must be attached to a copy of the notice of dishonor and must be substantially in the following form (RCW 62A.3-522):

AFFIDAVIT OF SERVICE BY MAIL

I, _____, hereby certify that on the _____ day of _____ (month), _____ (year), a copy of the foregoing Notice was served on _____ by mailing via the United States Postal Service, postage prepaid, at _____, Washington.

Dated: _____

_____ (Signature)

The person enforcing the check must retain the affidavit with the check but must also file a copy of the affidavit with the clerk of the court in which an action on the check is commenced (RCW 62A.3-522).

## Fees for Notary Services

**Maximum Fees.** The following maximum fees are authorized for Washington Notaries (WAC 308-30-020[1]):

- **Acknowledgments — $10.** For taking an acknowledgment, the Notary may charge $10.

- **Certified Copies — $10.** For certifying a copy, the Notary may charge $10.

- **Oaths and Affirmations — $10.** For administering an oath or affirmation, the Notary may charge $10.

- **Verification Upon Oath or Affirmation — $10.** For taking a verification upon an oath or affirmation, the Notary may charge $10.

- **Witnessing or Attesting a Signature — $10.** For witnessing or attesting a signature, the Notary may charge $10.

- **Certifying an Event or Act — $10.** For certifying that an event has occurred or an act has been performed, the Notary may charge $10.

- **Protests — $10.** For protesting a negotiable instrument, the Notary may charge $10.

**Notarial Acts for Remotely Located Individuals.** A Notary may charge a maximum fee of twenty-five dollars to perform a remote notarial act (WAC 308-30-220[6]).

**Travel Fees.** A Washington Notary may charge a fee for travel only if (WAC 308-30-020[4]):

- The Notary and the person requesting the notarial act agree upon the travel fee in advance of the travel.

- The Notary explains to the person requesting the notarial act that the travel fee is in addition to the notarial fee and is not required by law.

**Copying Fees.** For copying any document, a Notary may charge the actual cost of copying the document (WAC 308-30-220[4]).

**Option Not to Charge.** Notaries are not required to charge for their notarial services (WAC 308-30-220[3]). They also may charge any fee less than the statutory maximum.

**Overcharging.** Charging more than the prescribed maximum fees is considered "requesting unlawful compensation," a class C felony (RCW 9A.68.020).

## Unauthorized Acts

**Marriages.** Washington Notaries are not authorized to perform marriages unless they are also members of the clergy or officials authorized to solemnize nuptials. ∎

# Recordkeeping

## Journal of Notarial Acts

**Required.** A Notary Public must maintain a journal in which the Notary Public chronicles all notarial acts that the Notary Public performs (RCW 42.45.180[1]).

**Journal Entries.** For each notarization, a journal entry must be made at the same time as the performance of the notarization and contain the following information (RCW 42.45.180[4]):

- The date and time of the notarial act.

- A description of the record (e.g., deed of trust or affidavit of loss), if any, and type of notarial act (e.g., acknowledgment or verification upon oath or affirmation).

- The full name and address of each individual for whom the notarial act was performed.

- Any additional information as required by the director in rule.

**Tangible Journal Requirements.** A paper journal must have the capacity to record the following (WAC 308-30-200[1][b]):

- The information required by RCW 42.45.180(4).

- A description of the Notary's method of identifying the principal.

- The principal's signature, or the signature of an authorized party, or a notation in the notary journal that the notarial act was performed via remote notarization.

**Document Dates.** If the document has a specific date on it, the Notary should record that date in the journal of notarial acts.

Often the only date on a document is the date of the signature that is being notarized. If the signature is undated, however, the document may have no date on it at all. In that case, the Notary should record "no date" or "undated" in the journal.

For acknowledgments, the date the document was signed must either precede or be the same as the date of the notarization; it may not follow it. For a verification upon oath or affirmation, the date the document was signed and the date of the notarization must be the same.

A document whose signature is dated after the date on its Notary certificate risks rejection by a recorder, who may question how the document could have been notarized before it was signed.

**Method of Identification.** Although recording the method used to identify each signer is not required by law, it is prudent to do so.

If the signer is personally known, the Notary should indicate that in the journal. If the signer is identified using an ID document, the Notary should record the document's issuer, type, serial number, and date of issuance or expiration. If the signer is identified by a credible identifying witness, the Notary should record the witness's printed name and address and have the witness sign the journal.

**Journal Signature.** Perhaps the most important entry to obtain is the signer's signature. A journal signature protects the Notary against claims that a signer did not appear and is a deterrent to forgery, because it provides evidence of the signer's identity and appearance before the Notary.

To check for possible forgery, the Notary should compare the signature that the person leaves in the journal of notarial acts with the signatures on the document and on any IDs presented. The signatures should be at least reasonably similar.

The Notary also should observe the signing of the journal. If the signer appears to be laboring over the journal signature, this may be an indication of forgery in progress.

Since a journal signature is not required by law, the Notary may not refuse to notarize if the signer declines to leave one.

**Additional Entries.** Notaries may include additional information in their journals that is pertinent to a given notarization. For example, many Notaries enter the telephone number of all of the other signers and witnesses, as well as the address where the notarization was performed if not at the Notary's office. A description of the document signer's demeanor (e.g., "The signer appeared very nervous") or notations about the identity of other persons who were present for the notarization may also be pertinent.

One important entry to include is the signer's representative capacity — whether the signer is acting as attorney in fact, trustee, guardian, corporate officer or in another capacity — if not signing on his or her own behalf.

**Complete Entry Before Certificate.** The prudent Notary completes the journal entry before filling out the Notary certificate on a document. This prevents the signer from suddenly leaving with the notarized document before vital information can be entered in the journal.

**Journal-Entry Copies.** A Notary's official journal is a public record. Accordingly, if any person submits a written request specifying the month and year of a particular notarization, the type of document and the name(s) of the signer(s), the Notary may provide that person with a photocopy of the particular entry in the journal — but of no other entries. Adjacent entries should be covered before the photocopy is made.

The National Notary Association discourages "fishing expeditions" through the Notary journal by persons who are not able to be specific about the entry they are seeking.

**Journal Security.** The journal must be kept in a locked and secured area, under the direct and exclusive control of the Notary. Failure to secure the journal may be cause for the director to take administrative action against the Notary's commission (RCW 42.45.180[5]).

Notaries should never surrender control of their journals to anyone, unless required by law. Even when an employer has paid for the Notary's journal, it goes with the Notary upon termination of employment (WAC 308-30-200[3]). No one but the Notary can lawfully possess and use this official tool of office.

**Lost or Stolen Journal.** If a Notary's journal is lost or stolen, the Notary must promptly notify the Department of Licensing on discovering that the journal is lost or stolen. The National Notary Association recommends that this notification is made by certified mail.

**Disposition of Notary Journal.** A Notary must retain the journal for ten years after the performance of the last notarial act recorded in the journal. The journal is to be destroyed upon completion of the ten-year period (RCW 42.45.180[1]). ■

# Notary Certificate and Stamp

**Notary Certificate**

**Requirement.** In notarizing any document, a Notary must complete a Notary certificate (RCW 42.45.130[1]). The certificate is wording that indicates exactly what the Notary has certified. The Notary certificate may be typed or printed on the document itself or on an attachment.

The certificate must (RCW 42.45.130[1]), (RCW 42.45.130[2][b]) and (RCW 42.45.130[3]:

a. Be executed contemporaneously with the performance of the notarial act;

b. Be signed and dated by the Notary in the same manner as on file with the department;

c. Identify the jurisdiction in which the notarial act is performed;

d. Contain the title "Notary Public";

e. Be written in English or in dual languages, one of which must be English; and

f. Indicate the Notary's commission expiration date (RCW 42.45.130[1]).

g. For tangible documents an official stamp must be affixed to or embossed on the certificate. For electronic records, an official stamp must be attached to or logically associated with the certificate.

**Completing the Certificate.** When filling in the blanks in the Notary certificate, Notaries should either type or print neatly in dark ink.

It is not necessary to select or cross out variable terms such as "he/she/they," "is/are" or a plural "(s)."

**Correcting a Certificate.** When filling out the certificate, the Notary needs to make sure any preprinted information is accurate. For example, the venue — the state and county in which the notarial act is taking place — may have been filled in prior to the notarization. If the preprinted venue is incorrect, the Notary must line through the incorrect state and/or county, write in the proper site of the notarization, and initial and date the change.

**Certificate Forms.** Whenever possible, the notarial certificate should be on one page and should be incorporated as part of the document being notarized. If the notarial certificate is on its own page, or is separate from the rest of the document, The Washington State Department of Licensing recommends the Notary indicate on both the document being notarized and the certificate that the certificate is attached as a separate page (NPG).

When certificate wording is not preprinted on the document, or when preprinted wording is not acceptable, the Notary may attach a certificate form. This form typically is stapled to the document's left margin following the signature page. If the certificate form is replacing unacceptable preprinted wording, the Notary should line through the preprinted wording and write below it, "See attached certificate."

To prevent a certificate form from being removed and fraudulently placed on another document, the Notary may add a brief description of the document to the certificate: "This certificate is attached to a _____ (title or type of document), dated _____ (date), of _____ (number) pages, signed by _____ (name[s] of signers[s])."

The National Notary Association offers certificate forms that have similar wording preprinted on them; otherwise, the Notary will have to print, type, or stamp this information on each certificate form used. Finally, when Notaries attach a certificate form to a document, they always should note in their journals that they did so, as well as the means by which they attached the certificate to the document: "Certificate form stapled to document, following signature page."

While fraud-deterrent steps such as these can make it much more difficult for a certificate form to be removed and misused, there is no absolute protection against its removal and misuse. While a certificate form remains in their control, however, Notaries must absolutely ensure that it is attached only to its intended document.

**Selecting Certificates.** Washington law prohibits nonattorney Notaries from selecting Notary certificates for any transaction (WAC 308-30-090).

It is not the role of a nonattorney Notary to decide what type of certificate — and thus what type of notarization — a document needs. As ministerial officials, Notaries generally follow instructions and complete forms that have been provided for them; they do not issue instructions or decide which forms are appropriate in a given case.

If a document is presented to a Notary without certificate wording and if the signer does not know what type of notarial act is appropriate, the signer must be asked to find out what kind of notarization and certificate are needed. Usually the agency that issued or will be accepting the document can provide this information. A Notary who selects certificates is engaging in the unauthorized practice of law.

**Do Not Pre-Sign or Pre-Seal Certificates.** A Notary must never sign or seal certificates ahead of time or permit other persons to attach a Notary certificate form to a document. A Notary may not sign a certificate until the notarial act is performed (RCW 42.45.130[6]).

A Notary must never give or mail an unattached, signed and sealed certificate form to another person and trust that person to attach it to a particular document, even if asked to do so by a signer who previously appeared before the Notary.

These actions could facilitate fraud or forgery, and, since such actions would be indefensible in a civil court of law, they could subject the Notary to lawsuits to recover damages resulting from the Notary's neglect or misconduct.

**Certificates Must Be Page-Size.** If appropriate Notary certificate wording is not printed or typed on the document itself, a certificate form may be attached only if it is on a sheet exactly the same size as the document's other pages and is fastened in the same manner as the other pages. Documents with attached Notary certificates that are less than a full page in size will be rejected by the county auditor.

In addition, no document page or Notary certificate may be larger than 8½ by 14 inches (RCW 65.04.045[2]).

**Certificates Must Have One-Inch Margin.** Any document presented for recording in Washington must have a one-inch margin on the top, bottom and sides of all pages, except for the first page, which must have a top margin of at least three inches (RCW 65.04.045[2]). Thus, any Notary certificate attached to a recordable document must not only be page-sized but must also have a top, bottom and side margin of at least one inch.

County auditors will permit a Notary's seal, incidental writing or a minor portion of a signature to protrude into the margin. Such instances will not affect a document's recording (RCW 65.04.045[2]).

**Type Not Less than Eight Points.** No page or Notary certificate may contain printing smaller than eight points (RCW 65.04.045[2]).

**Documents Not Recorded in Washington.** Pages and Notary certificates on documents that will not be recorded in Washington by a county auditor may not need to adhere to specified format requirements. However, to avoid an unintentional mistake, the National Notary Association encourages Washington Notaries to consistently use certificates that adhere to this format regardless of where the signer intends to have the document recorded.

**False Certificate.** A Notary Public who knowingly creates or completes a false Notary certificate is guilty of a gross misdemeanor (RCW 42.20.050 and 42.44.160).

**Notary Stamp**

**Requirement.** Washington law requires Notaries to affix an official stamp on every tangible notarial certificate (RCW 42.45.130[2][a]).

**Format.** The Notary seal may be either an inked-stamp seal or an embossing seal. An inked-stamp seal may be either rectangular or circular. The imprint of an inked-stamp seal must be affixed with indelible ink and may not be preprinted on the certificate. The face of an inked-stamp seal must contain permanently affixed letters and numerals.

An embossing seal must be circular and a minimum of 1 5/8 inches in diameter (WAC 308-30-010). On recordable documents, the impression made by an embossing seal must be capable of photographic reproduction (RCW 65.04.045[2]).

**Required Information.** The Notary seal must contain the following elements, all printed in not less than eight-point type (RCW 42.44.050 and WAC 308-30-010):

- The Notary Public's name as it appears on the commission.

- The words "Notary Public" and "State of Washington."

- The Notary's commission expiration date.

**Notary Commission Number.** The Washington Administrative code also requires the official stamp to include the Notary Public's commission number (WAC 308-30-070[1][e]).

**Use of Expired Seal Prohibited.** Use of a Notary's seal with an expired date is expressly prohibited by law (WAC 308-30-130).

**Placement of the Seal Impression.** The Notary's official seal should be affixed near, but not over, the Notary's signature on the Notary certificate.

If there is no room for the seal, the Notary may have no choice but to complete and attach a certificate form that duplicates the notarial wording on the document.

**L.S.** On many certificates the letters "L.S." appear, indicating where the seal is to be located. These letters abbreviate the Latin term *locus sigilli*, meaning "place of the seal." An inking seal should be placed near but not over the letters, so that wording imprinted by the seal will not be obscured. An embossing seal may be placed directly over the letters, slightly displacing portions of the characters and leaving a clue that document examiners can use to distinguish an original from a forged photocopy.

**Illegible Seal.** If an initial seal impression is unreadable and there is ample room on the document, another impression can be affixed nearby. The illegibility of the first impression will indicate why a second seal impression was necessary. The Notary should then record in the journal that a second impression was applied.

A Notary should never attempt to fix an imperfect seal impression with pen, ink or correction fluid. This may be viewed as evidence of tampering and cause the document to be rejected by a receiving agency.

**Authorization to Purchase Seal.** When a Notary application has been approved, the Department of Licensing sends the new Notary a Certificate of Commission, a photocopy of which authorizes purchase of the required Notary seal (RCW 42.44.050).

**Unauthorized Manufacture of Seal.** It is unlawful to manufacture, give, sell, buy or possess a Notary seal if the Department of Licensing has not issued a Certificate of Commission (RCW 42.44.050).

Further, a vendor may not provide a Notary seal to a Notary unless the Notary presents a photocopy of the Certificate of Commission (WAC 308-30-010[6] and [7]).

**Lost or Stolen Seal.** If a Notary's seal is lost or stolen, the Notary must notify the Department of Licensing.

The notice must state that the seal has been lost or stolen, and it must be signed by the Notary. The Notary may then obtain a replacement seal which must contain some variance from the original seal. (If only initials were used on the original, for example, the full name could be used on the replacement seal.)

If the original seal is found or recovered after another has been obtained, the original must be surrendered to the Department of Licensing (WAC 308-30-050).

**Disposition of Notary Seal.** When a Notary resigns, or upon revocation or expiration of the commission, the Notary seal must be disabled by destroying, defacing, damaging it in manner that makes it unusable.

Should the Notary die during the commission term, the Notary's personal representative should destroy the seal.

**Never Surrender Seal.** The Notary seal is the exclusive property of the Notary named on it and must not be used by any other person or surrendered to an employer upon termination of the Notary's employment, even if the employer paid for it (RCW 42.44.090[4]). ■

# In-Person Electronic Notarization and Remote Online Notarization

**Purpose.** Electronic commerce produces a need for Notaries to witness electronic transactions, just as Notaries have witnessed paper transactions for centuries. While the tools for creating and signing documents may be different, the impartial witnessing services of a Notary remain the same and are as important as ever. Notaries who are endorsed by the Department of Licensing with an electronic records and/or remote Notary Public endorsement may now perform notarizations for in-person electronic transactions and remotely located individuals (Washington Senate Bill 5641).

## In-Person Electronic Notarizations and Remote Online Notarizations Defined

**In-Person Electronic Notarization.** In-person electronic notarization, also called IPEN or eNotarization, still requires the Notary and signer to meet face-to-face and be physically in the same room. Similar to pen and paper notarizations, the Notary must identify the signer through personal knowledge or satisfactory evidence, screen the signer for willingness and awareness, and certify the facts for the requested notarization. However, for electronic notarizations, the document is presented electronically, such as on a computer or tablet, and the signature will be affixed electronically by the signer. The Notary certificate will be provided at the end of the document or logically attached to the document for the Notary to complete and affix the electronic signature and the electronic seal. And of course, a journal record is made.

**Remote Online Notarization.** Only Notaries who apply for and receive a remote Notary endorsement from the Department of Licensing may perform Remote Online Notarizations. Remote Online Notarization, also referred to as RON, may be performed when the Notary and signer cannot meet face-to-face in the same room. RON requires the Notary and signer to meet via audio-video technology that allows them to see and hear each other in real-time. The electronic record or document and the electronic Notary certificate are uploaded to a shared platform by a Notary technology provider, and the notarization takes place via that platform.

The Notary would still follow the fundamental steps for the notarization. The Notary screens the signer for identity, willingness and awareness and certifies the facts for the requested notarization. Then the Notary completes the electronic certificate and affixes an electronic signature and stamp. In addition to creating a journal record for the transaction, an audio-video recording of the transaction is required.

**Authorized Acts.** A Notary Public who has received an electronic records Notary Public endorsement from the department may perform the following electronic notarial acts (WAC 308-30-120):

1. Taking an acknowledgment;
2. Taking a verification on oath or affirmation;
3. Witnessing or attesting a signature;
4. Certifying or attesting a copy;
5. Certifying that an event has occurred or an act has been performed; and

6. Noting a protest of a negotiable instrument, if the Notary Public is:

   a. Licensed to practice law in the state of Washington;

   b. Acting under the authority of an attorney who is licensed to practice law in this or another state; or

   c. Acting under the authority of a financial institution regulated by this state, another state, or the federal government.

## Becoming an Electronic Records or Remote Notary Public

**Special Endorsements Required.** A Notary may not perform acts on electronic records unless the Notary holds an electronic records and/or a remote Notary Public endorsement (WAC 308-30-030).

Before an electronic or remote Notary performs an electronic or remote notarial act, the Notary must complete an application form and pay the prescribed fee. In addition to submitting an application and fee, the Notary must also provide to the Department of Licencing within 30 days of applying, the information for the approved technology and technology providers with which they have enrolled.

An applicant may only apply for a remote Notary endorsement if: (a) They currently hold an active Notary commission with an electronic records Notary endorsement; (b) They currently hold an active Notary commission, and are applying for an electronic records Notary endorsement and a remote Notary endorsement simultaneously; or (c) They are applying for a Notary commission, an electronic records Notary endorsement, and a remote notarial acts endorsement simultaneously.

**Term and Renewal.** The electronic records and remote Notary endorsements continue for as long as the Notary's commission is valid. Renewal would require the same process.

**Termination of Commission or Endorsement.** The department may take action against the commission and/or endorsement of a Notary who fails to comply with these rules as provided in RCW 42.45.210,

42.45.270, and chapter 18.235 RCW. Any restriction, suspension, or revocation of a Notary's commission will automatically have the same effect on any endorsement the Notary holds (WAC 308-30-27).

A Notary may terminate their Notary commission and/or electronic records endorsement or remote Notary endorsement by notifying the department of this intent in writing and disposing of all or any part of a tamper-evident technology in the Notary's control whose purpose was to perform electronic notarizations.

A Notary may terminate the electronic records and/or the remote Notary endorsement and maintain the underlying Notary commission.

A Notary whose commission is terminated or expired, either by the Notary or the department, must disable their official stamp by destroying, defacing, damaging, or securing the device against use. The Notary must maintain their notarial journals for ten years as required by RCW 42.45.180 and WAC 308-30-210.

## Electronic Signature

**Technology Requirements.** A Notary's electronic signature must use tamper evident technology. This means that any changes made to the document after the electronic signature has been applied would be evident (WAC 308-30-020). The Notary's electronic signature must also be capable of independent verification. These requirements are typically fulfilled by using a digital certificate.

**Security.** The Notary must take reasonable steps to ensure that no other individual may possess or access the Notary's electronic signature. Access to the system must be secured with password protection or other means of authentication. The technology must remain under the Notary's sole control (WAC 308-30-170). If the technology does not meet the requirements of the Washington rules or is a technology that the Notary is uncertain as to how to use, the Notary must refuse to provide the service (WAC 308-30-140).

## Electronic Stamp

**Requirements.** An electronic stamp must be a digital image that appears in the likeness or representation of a traditional physical official stamp. The electronic stamp is used to authenicate the electronic notarial act and must be affixed or logically associated with the electronic notarial certificate (WAC 308-30-180).

**Security.** As with the traditional physical Notary stamp, the electronic stamp is the exclusive property of the Notary and must not be used by any other individual. It should be secured with a password or other means of authentication.

### Electronic Journal

**Requirements.** A tangible journal is required for all notarizations. Notaries performing remote notarization are not required to collect and maintain the signatures of the signers when those notarizations are performed remotely. Notaries must note in their tangible Notary log that a notarization was performed remotely.

An electronic journal may also be kept and must (a) be maintained only in addition to the tangible journal; (b) have the capacity to record the information required for a tangible notarial journal; (b) enable access by a password or other secure means of authentication; (d) be tamper-evident; (e) create a duplicate record of the journal as a backup; and (f) be capable of providing tangible or electronic copies of any entry made in the journal (WAC 308-30-200).

**Access.** A Notary or the Notary's personal representative is required to provide access instructions to the Department of Licensing for any electronic journal maintained or stored by the Notary upon commission resignation, revocation, or expiration without renewal, or upon the death or adjudicated incompetence of the Notary.

**Disposition.** Ten years after the performance of the last notarial act chronicled in an electronic journal, the journal is to be destroyed by deleting any remaining records pertaining to the electronic journal and deleting any remaining tamper-evident technology in the Notary's possession.

## Additional RON Requirements

**Audio-Video Technology Requirements for RON.** Since a Remote Online Notarization requires the Notary and signer to be able to communicate through audio-video technology and to capture a recording of the transaction, there are additional considerations and requirements.

**Identification of the Remotely Located Individual.** The law states that the Notary must identify the signer through personal knowledge or the oath of a credible witness, or for a remote online notarization, another option is to use two different types of identity proofing. Typically, the technology provider will implement identity proofing even if the Notary personally knows the signer and/or uses a credible witness. Identity proofing is accomplished by analyzing the signer's ID through credential analysis software and asking the signer to answer knowledge-based authentication questions.

1. **Credential Analysis:** Credential analysis is the process by which the government-issued identification card of the principal is validated. The process requires a third party to use technology confirming the security features on an ID and that the ID is not fraudulent. The third party also uses information available from the issuing source or other authoritative source to confirm the details on the credential. As part of the process, the third party is required to provide an output of the authenticity test to the Notary and enable the Notary to visually compare the credential used during credential analysis with the principal who has personally appeared before the Notary via audio-visual transmission.

2. **Knowledge Based Authentication:** KBA is a method of authentication which seeks to prove the identity of someone accessing a service such as a financial institution or website. As the name suggests, Knowledge Based Authentication requires the knowledge of private information of the individual to prove that the person providing the identity information is the owner of the identity. There are two types of KBA: Static KBA, which is based on a pre-agreed set of shared secrets, and Dynamic KBA, which is based on questions generated from a wider base of personal information.

Electronic Notarization

**Verification of the Record to be Notarized.** For a RON transaction, the Notary Public must be able to reasonably confirm that a record presented to the Notary is the same record in which the remotely located individual made a statement or on which the individual executed a signature.

**Audiovisual Recording.** In addition to recording a journal entry as required for traditional notarizations, an electronic records Notary or a person acting on behalf of the electronic records Notary, must create an industry standard audiovisual recording of the performance of the notarial act. The audiovisual recording must be retained by the Notary or technology provider for at least ten years from the date of the recording.

**Signers Located Outside of US.** If the remotely located individual is outside the United States at the time of notarization, the Notary must ensure that the record: (a) is to be filed with or relates to a matter before a public official or court, governmental entity, or other entity subject to the jurisdiction of the United States or (b) involves property located in the territorial jurisdiction of the United States or involves a transaction substantially connected with the United States; and the act of making the statement or signing the record is not prohibited by the foreign state in which the remotely located individual is located.

**Notarial Certificate Language Requirement.** As with all notarizations, the Notary must complete, sign and stamp a Notary certificate for the transaction. When completing a Notary certificate for a remote online notarization, the certificate must indicate that the notarial act was performed using communication technology. In addition to the other requirements for the certificate stating the facts for the notarization, the certificate must also include a statement substantially as follows: "This notarial act involved the use of communication technology."

A short form of acknowledgment prescribed in RCW 42.45.140 satisfies the requirement of RCW 42.45.280(4) and 42.45.130 (1)(g) if it is in substantially one of the following forms for the purposes indicated:

a. For an acknowledgment in an individual capacity:

State of Washington

County of .......

This record was acknowledged before me by means of communication technology on (date) by (name(s) of individuals).

. . . .

(Signature of notary public)

Notary Public

(Electronic official stamp)

(My commission expires: . . . .)

b. For an acknowledgment in a representative capacity:

State of Washington

County of .......

This record was acknowledged before me by means of communication technology on (date) by (name(s) of individuals) as (type of authority, such as officer or trustee) of (name of party on behalf of whom the instrument was executed).

. . . .

(Signature of notary public)

Notary Public

(Electronic official stamp)

(My commission expires: . . . .)

c. For verification on oath or affirmation:

State of Washington

County of .......

Signed and sworn to (or affirmed) before me by means of communication technology on (date) by (name(s) of individuals making statement).

. . . .

(Signature of notary public)

Notary Public

(Electronic official stamp)

(My commission expires: . . . .)

d. For witnessing or attesting a signature:

State of Washington

County of .......

Signed or attested before me by means of communication technology on (date) by (name(s) of individuals).

. . . .

(Signature of notary public)

Notary Public

(Electronic official stamp)

(My commission expires: . . . .)

**Fees for Remote Notarial Acts.** An approved and endorsed remote online Notary may charge a maximum fee of twenty-five dollars to perform a remote notarial act. ■

# Misconduct, Fines and Penalties

## Misconduct

**Misconduct Defined.** A Notary is guilty of official misconduct if, with intent to obtain a benefit or to deprive another person of a lawful right or privilege, he or she intentionally commits an unauthorized act or intentionally refrains from performing a required duty (RCW 9A.80.010[1]).

## Restriction of Commission

**Denial of Application.** The Department of Licensing may deny a Notary application for reasons that include (RCW 42.44.030):

- Unprofessional conduct specified in RCW 18.235.130 (see below).

- Disciplinary action taken against any professional license in Washington or any other state.

- Engaging in official misconduct as defined under RCW 42.44.160(1) (issuing a false Notary certificate knowing that the contents of the certificate are false), whether or not criminal penalties resulted.

- A violation of any of the provisions of RCW 19.154, relating to immigration services fraud. (See "Immigration Services Fraud Prevention Act," pages 18–20.)

An application for a Notary commission also may be denied for unprofessional conduct as defined in RCW 18.235.130. The following fifteen conditions constitute unprofessional conduct according to that statute:

- Any act involving moral turpitude, dishonesty, or corruption relating to the practice of the person's profession or operation of the person's business.

- Misrepresentation or concealment of a material fact in obtaining, renewing or reinstatement of a license.

- False, deceptive or misleading advertising.

- Incompetence, negligence or malpractice that results in harm or damage to another or that creates an unreasonable risk of harm or damage to another.

- Suspension, revocation, or restriction of a license to engage in any business or profession by competent authority in any state, federal or foreign jurisdiction.

- Failure to cooperate with the disciplinary authority in the course of an investigation, audit or inspection authorized by law.

- Failure to comply with an order issued by the disciplinary authority.

- Violating any of the provisions of this chapter or the chapters specified in RCW 18.235.020(2) or any rules made by the disciplinary authority under the chapters specified in RCW 18.235.020(2).

- Aiding or abetting an unlicensed person to practice or operate a business or profession when a license is required.

- Practice or operation of a business or profession beyond the scope of practice or operation as defined by law or rule.

- Misrepresentation in any aspect of the conduct of the business or profession.

- Failure to adequately supervise or oversee staff, whether employees or contractors, to the extent that consumers may be harmed or damaged.

- Conviction of any gross misdemeanor or felony relating to the practice of the person's profession or operation of the person's business.

- Interference with an investigation or disciplinary action.

- Engaging in unlicensed practice without holding a valid, unexpired, unrevoked and unsuspended license to do so or as further defined in RCW 18.235.010.

- A fraudulent, dishonest, or deceitful misstatement or omission in the application for a commission as a notary public submitted to the department.

- A conviction of the applicant or notary public of any felony or crime involving fraud, dishonesty, or deceit.

- A finding against, or admission of liability by, the applicant or notary public in any legal proceeding or disciplinary action based on the applicant's or notary public's fraud, dishonesty or deceit.

- Failure by the notary public to discharge any duty required of a notary public, whether by this chapter, rules of the director, or any federal or state law.

- Use of false or misleading advertising or representation by the notary public representing that the notary public has a duty, right, or privilege that the notary public does not have.

- Violation by the Notary Public of a rule of the director regarding a Notary Public.

- Denial, refusal to renew, revocation, suspension, or conditioning of a notary public commission in another state.

- Failure of the notary public to maintain an assurance (bond) as required by law.

- Making or noting a protest of a negotiable instrument without being a person authorized by law.

**Revocation of Commission.** The Department of Licensing may revoke a Notary's commission if the Notary is found incompetent by a court. In this case, the Notary's guardian or conservator must deliver a letter of resignation within 30 days of judgment to the Department of Licensing on behalf of the Notary. The letter must be accompanied by the Notary's seal (RCW 42.44.170 and WAC 308-30-040).

**Forced Resignation of Commission.** Washington Notaries are required to resign their commission in two situations: if they cease to live or, if nonresident, to be regularly employed in Washington; and if they no longer are able to read or write English (WAC 308-30-150).

**Must Report Conviction.** Within 30 days of having been convicted of a felony or lesser offense — such as falsifying records, false swearing and giving false information, etc. — the Notary must file a written statement with the Department of Licensing. The statement must contain: the Notary's name, commission number and commission expiration date; the type of conviction and sentence; and the court and jurisdiction in which the Notary was convicted. Judgments against the Notary for any civil action must also be reported (WAC 308-30-140).

### Illegal and Improper Acts

**Official Misconduct.** A Notary who engages in official misconduct, such as that defined under RCW 18.235.130 (unprofessional conduct) or a violation of RCW 19.154 (immigration services fraud), is guilty of a gross misdemeanor (RCW 9A.80.010[2], 42.20.090 and 42.44.160[2]).

**Impersonating a Notary.** A person who does not have a valid Notary commission or who impersonates a Notary is guilty of a gross misdemeanor (RCW 42.44.160[3]).

**Unauthorized Manufacture of Seal.** It is unlawful to manufacture, give, sell, buy or possess a Notary seal if the Department of Licensing has not issued a Certificate of Commission (RCW 42.44.050).

Further, a vendor may not provide a Notary seal to a Notary unless the Notary presents a photocopy of the Certificate of Commission (WAC 308-30-010[6] and [7]).

**Unauthorized Practice of Law.** A Notary who engages in the unauthorized practice of law is guilty of a gross misdemeanor for the first offense. Each subsequent violation is a class C felony (RCW 2.48.180[3]). (See "Unauthorized Practice of Law," pages 16–17.)

**Notarize Own Signature.** Notaries may not notarize a document in which they are a signer (RCW 42.44.080[10]). This means that Notaries may never notarize their own signatures and, in most cases, that they may not notarize documents in which they are named.

**False Certificate.** A Notary who knowingly completes a false Notary certificate — for example, by stating a signer appeared when he or she actually did not — is guilty of a gross misdemeanor (RCW 42.20.050 and 42.44.160[1]).

**False Document.** A Notary who falsely completes a document — for example, by filling in a document's blank spaces — is guilty of forgery with intent to deceive or defraud, a class C felony (RCW 9A.60.020).

**Failure to Require Personal Appearance.** A Notary may not notarize any document without the signer personally appearing before the Notary (RCW 42.44.080[1] through [4]). Since Notary certificate wording specifies that the signer appeared before the Notary at the time of notarization, failing to require such personal appearance is considered completion of a false certificate, a gross misdemeanor under Washington's law (RCW 42.20.050 and 42.44.160[1]).

**Endorsements and Testimonials.** Notaries may not use their seals or the title Notary Public to promote or endorse any product, service, contest, candidate or other offering (WAC 308-30-160).

**Overcharging.** A Notary may not charge more than the maximum fees allowed by law. Charging more than the prescribed maximum fees is considered "requesting unlawful compensation," a class C felony (RCW 9A.68.020).

**Fees Not Posted.** Notaries must post the notarization fee schedule in a conspicuous area in their place of business, or present it to each customer outside their business, in no smaller than 10-point type (WAC 308-30-020).

**Signature Under Duress.** No person, including a Notary, may force a person to sign a document. A person is guilty of obtaining a signature by deception or duress, a class C felony, if, by intending to deceive or defraud, he or she causes the signer to execute an instrument (RCW 9A.60.030).

**Duty Performed by Another for Profit.** No public officer may willingly grant authority to, or accept a fee from, another person who intends to exercise the duties of that public office (RCW 42.20.020).

### Appeal of Denial or Revocation

**Procedure.** Should a Notary wish to appeal a denial or revocation of his or her commission, he or she must submit a notice in writing and mail or deliver it to the Department of Licensing. The written notice of appeal must be received by the Department within 20 days of the date of denial or revocation, or the applicant will lose the right to appeal (WAC 308-30-080). ■

# Washington Laws Pertaining to Notaries Public

Reprinted on the following pages is the complete text of the enacted laws and administrative regulations affecting Notaries and notarial acts, drawn from the Revised Code of Washington (RCW) and the Washington Administrative Code (WAC). Citations in brackets at the end of each section indicate the legislative history of the section.

**Chapter 42.45 RCW**

**REVISED UNIFORM LAW ON NOTARIAL ACTS**

**Sections**

| | |
|---|---|
| 42.45.010 | Definitions. |
| 42.45.020 | Authority to perform notarial act. |
| 42.45.030 | Certain notarial acts—Requirements. |
| 42.45.040 | Personal appearance. |
| 42.45.050 | Identification of individual. |
| 42.45.060 | Refusal to perform notarial act. |
| 42.45.070 | Individual unable to sign—Signature. |
| 42.45.080 | Notarial act in this state. |

42.45.090   Notarial act in another state—Effect in this state.
42.45.100   Notarial act under authority of federally recognized Indian tribe.
42.45.110   Notarial act under federal authority.
42.45.120   Foreign notarial act.
42.45.130   Certificate of notarial act.
42.45.140   Short form certificates.
42.45.150   Official stamp.
42.45.160   Stamping device—Security.
42.45.170   Fees.
42.45.180   Journal.
42.45.190   Notarial acts on electronic records—Technology—Notification—Standards.
42.45.200   Commission—Qualifications—Oath—Surety bond—Commission term—Electronic records notary public.
42.45.210   Grounds to deny, refuse to renew, revoke, suspend, or condition commission of notary public.
42.45.220   Database of notaries public.
42.45.230   Prohibited acts.
42.45.240   Validity of notarial acts.
42.45.250   Rules.
42.45.260   Commissions in effect July 1, 2018—Continuation.
42.45.270   Uniform regulation of business and professions act—Application.
42.45.280   Electronic records notary public.
42.45.900   Short title.
42.45.901   Application.
42.45.902   Savings.
42.45.903   Application—Construction.
42.45.904   Relation to electronic signatures in global and national commerce act.
42.45.905   Effective date—2017 c 281.

**RCW 42.45.010 Definitions**

In this chapter:

(1) "Acknowledgment" means a declaration by an individual in the presence of a notarial officer stating that the individual has signed a record of the individual's free will for the purpose stated in the record and, if the record is signed in a representative capacity, the individual also declares that he or she signed the record with proper authority and signed it as the act of the individual or entity identified in the record.

(2) "Department" means the department of licensing.

(3) "Director" means the director of licensing or the director's designee.

(4) "Electronic" means relating to technology having electrical, digital, magnetic, wireless, optical, electromagnetic, or similar capabilities.

(5) "Electronic records notary public" means an individual commissioned by the director to perform a notarial act with respect to electronic records. Nothing in chapter 281, Laws of 2017 authorizes an electronic records notary public to provide court reporting services.

(6) "Electronic signature" means an electronic symbol, sound, or process attached to or logically associated with a record and executed or adopted by an individual with the intent to sign the record.

(7) "In a representative capacity" means acting as:

(a) An authorized officer, agent, partner, trustee, or other representative for a person other than an individual;

(b) A public officer, personal representative, guardian, or other representative, in the capacity stated in a record;

(c) An agent or attorney-in-fact for a principal; or

(d) An authorized representative of another in any other capacity.

(8) "Notarial act" means an act, whether performed with respect to a tangible or electronic record, that a notarial officer may perform under the law of this state. The term includes taking an acknowledgment, administering an oath or affirmation, taking a verification on oath or affirmation, witnessing or attesting a signature, certifying or attesting a copy, certifying the occurrence of an event or the performance of an act, and noting a protest of a negotiable instrument if the protest was prepared under the authority of an attorney licensed to practice law in this state or another state, or was prepared under the authority of a financial institution that is regulated by this state, another state, or the federal government.

(9) "Notarial officer" means a notary public or other individual authorized to perform a notarial act.

(10) "Notary public" means an individual commissioned to perform a notarial act by the director.

(11) "Official stamp" means a physical image affixed to or embossed on a tangible record or an electronic image attached to or logically associated with an electronic record.

(12) "Person" means an individual, corporation, business trust, statutory trust, estate, trust, partnership, limited liability company, association, joint venture, public corporation, government or governmental subdivision, agency, or instrumentality, or any other legal or commercial entity.

(13) "Record" means information that is inscribed on a tangible medium or that is stored in an electronic or other medium and is retrievable in human perceivable form.

(14) "Sign" means, with present intent to authenticate or adopt a record:

(a) To execute or adopt a tangible symbol; or

(b) To attach to or logically associate with the record an electronic symbol, sound, or process.

(15) "Signature" means a tangible symbol or an electronic signature that evidences the signing of a record.

(16) "Stamping device" means:

(a) A physical device capable of affixing to or embossing on a tangible record an official stamp; or

(b) An electronic device or process capable of attaching to or logically associating with an electronic record an official stamp.

(17) "State" means a state of the United States, the District of Columbia, Puerto Rico, the United States Virgin Islands, or any territory or insular possession subject to the jurisdiction of the United States.

(18) "Verification on oath or affirmation" means a declaration, made by an individual on oath or affirmation before a notarial officer, that a statement in a record is true.

[2017 c 281 § 2.]

### RCW 42.45.020 Authority to perform notarial act

(1) A notarial officer may perform a notarial act authorized by this chapter or by law of this state other than this chapter.

(2)(a) A notarial officer may not perform a notarial act with respect to a record to which the officer or the officer's spouse or domestic partner is a party, or in which any of the above have a direct beneficial interest.

(b) A notarial officer may not notarize the notarial officer's own signature.

(c) A notarial act performed in violation of this subsection (2) is voidable.

(3) A notarial officer may certify that a tangible copy of an electronic record is an accurate copy of the electronic record.

[2019 c 154 § 2; 2017 c 281 § 4.]

NOTES:

Effective date—2019 c 154: See note following RCW 42.45.280.

### RCW 42.45.030 Certain notarial acts—Requirements

(1) A notarial officer who takes an acknowledgment of a record shall determine, from personal knowledge or satisfactory evidence of the identity of the individual, that the individual appearing before the officer and making the acknowledgment has the identity claimed and that the signature on the record is the signature of the individual.

(2) A notarial officer who takes a verification of a statement on oath or affirmation shall determine, from personal knowledge or satisfactory evidence of the identity of the individual, that the individual appearing before the officer and making the verification has the identity claimed and that the signature on the statement verified is the signature of the individual.

(3) A notarial officer who witnesses or attests to a signature shall determine, from personal knowledge or satisfactory evidence of the identity of the individual, that the individual appearing before the officer and signing the record has the identity claimed.

(4) A notarial officer who certifies or attests a copy of a record or an item that was copied shall compare the copy with the original record or item and determine that the copy is a full, true, and accurate transcription or reproduction of the record or item.

(5) A notarial officer may make or note a protest of a negotiable instrument only if the notarial officer is licensed to practice law in this state, acting under the authority of an attorney who is licensed to practice law in this or another state, or acting under the authority of a financial institution regulated by this state, another state, or the federal

government. In making or noting a protest of a negotiable instrument the notarial officer or licensed attorney shall determine the matters set forth in RCW 62A.3-505(b).

[2017 c 281 § 5.]

### RCW 42.45.040 Personal appearance

Except as provided in RCW 42.45.280, if a notarial act relates to a statement made in or a signature executed on a record, the individual making the statement or executing the signature shall appear personally before the notarial officer.

[2019 c 154 § 3; 2017 c 281 § 6.]

NOTES:

Effective date—2019 c 154: See note following RCW 42.45.280.

### RCW 42.45.050 Identification of individual

(1) A notarial officer has personal knowledge of the identity of an individual appearing before the officer if the individual is personally known to the officer through dealings sufficient to provide reasonable certainty that the individual has the identity claimed.

(2) A notarial officer has satisfactory evidence of the identity of an individual appearing before the officer if the officer can identify the individual:

(a) By means of:

(i) A passport, driver's license, or government-issued nondriver identification card, which is current or expired not more than three years before performance of the notarial act; or

(ii) Another form of government identification issued to an individual, which is current or expired not more than three years before performance of the notarial act, contains the signature or a photograph of the individual, and is satisfactory to the officer; or

(b) By a verification on oath or affirmation of a credible witness personally appearing before the officer and personally known to the officer and who provides satisfactory evidence of his or her identity as described in (a) of this subsection.

(3) A notarial officer may require an individual to provide additional information or identification credentials necessary to assure the officer of the identity of the individual.

[2017 c 281 § 7.]

### RCW 42.45.060 Refusal to perform notarial act

(1) A notarial officer has the authority to refuse to perform a notarial act if the officer is not satisfied that:

(a) The individual executing the record is competent or has the capacity to execute the record; or

(b) The individual's signature is knowingly and voluntarily made.

(2) A notarial officer has the authority to refuse to perform a notarial act unless refusal is prohibited by law other than this chapter.

[2017 c 281 § 8.]

### RCW 42.45.070 Individual unable to sign—Signature

Except as otherwise provided in RCW 64.08.100, if an individual is physically unable to sign a record, the individual may direct an individual other than the notarial officer to sign the individual's name on the record. The notarial officer shall insert "signature affixed by (name of other individual) at the direction of (name of individual)" or words of similar import.

[2017 c 281 § 9.]

### RCW 42.45.080 Notarial act in this state

(1) A notarial act may be performed in this state by:

(a) A notary public of this state;

(b) A judge, clerk, or deputy clerk of a court of this state; or

(c) Any other individual authorized to perform the specific act by the law of this state.

(2) The signature and title of an individual authorized by chapter 281, Laws of 2017 to perform a notarial act in this state are prima facie evidence that the signature is genuine and that the individual holds the designated title.

(3) The signature and title of a notarial officer described in subsection (1)(a) or (b) of this section conclusively establishes the authority of the officer to perform the notarial act.

[2017 c 281 § 10.]

### RCW 42.45.090 Notarial act in another state—Effect in this state

(1) A notarial act performed in another state has the same effect under the law of this state as if performed by a notarial officer of this state, if the act performed in that state is performed by:

(a) A notary public of that state;

(b) A judge, clerk, or deputy clerk of a court of that state; or

(c) Any other individual authorized by the law of that state to perform the notarial act.

(2) The signature and title of an individual performing a notarial act in another state are prima facie evidence that the signature is genuine and that the individual holds the designated title.

(3) The signature and title of a notarial officer described in subsection (1)(a) through (c) of this section conclusively establishes the authority of the officer to perform the notarial act.

[2017 c 281 § 11.]

### RCW 42.45.100 Notarial act under authority of federally recognized Indian tribe

(1) A notarial act performed under the authority and in the jurisdiction of a federally recognized Indian tribe has the same effect as if performed by a notarial officer of this state, if the act performed in the jurisdiction of the tribe is performed by:

(a) A notary public of the tribe;

(b) A judge, clerk, or deputy clerk of a court of the tribe; or

(c) Any other individual authorized by the law of the tribe to perform the notarial act.

(2) The signature and title of an individual performing a notarial act under the authority of and in the jurisdiction of a federally recognized Indian tribe are prima facie evidence that the signature is genuine and that the individual holds the designated title.

(3) The signature and title of a notarial officer described in subsection (1)(a) through (c) of this section conclusively establishes the authority of the officer to perform the notarial act.

[2017 c 281 § 12.]

### RCW 42.45.110 Notarial act under federal authority

(1) A notarial act performed under federal law has the same effect under the law of this state as if performed by a notarial officer of this state, if the act performed under federal law is performed by:

(a) A judge, clerk, or deputy clerk of a court;

(b) An individual in military service or performing duties under the authority of military service who is authorized to perform notarial acts under federal law;

(c) An individual designated a notarizing officer by the United States department of state for performing notarial acts overseas; or

(d) Any other individual authorized by federal law to perform the notarial act.

(2) The signature and title of an individual acting under federal authority and performing a notarial act are prima facie evidence that the signature is genuine and that the individual holds the designated title.

(3) The signature and title of an officer described in subsection (1)(a), (b), or (c) of this section conclusively establishes the authority of the officer to perform the notarial act.

[2017 c 281 § 13.]

### RCW 42.45.120 Foreign notarial act

(1) In this section, "foreign state" means a government other than the United States, a state, or a federally recognized Indian tribe.

(2) If a notarial act is performed under the authority and in the jurisdiction of a foreign state or constituent unit of the foreign state or is performed under the authority of a multinational or international governmental organization, the act has the same effect under the law of this state as if performed by a notarial officer of this state.

(3) If the title of office and indication of authority to perform notarial acts in a foreign state appears in a digest of foreign law or in a list customarily used as a source for that information, the authority of an officer with that title to perform notarial acts is conclusively established.

(4) The signature and official stamp of an individual holding an office described in subsection (3) of this section are prima facie evidence that the signature is genuine and the individual holds the designated title.

(5) An apostille in the form prescribed by the Hague Convention of October 5, 1961, and issued by a foreign state party to the Hague Convention conclusively establishes that the signature of the notarial officer is genuine and that the officer holds the indicated office.

(6) A consular authentication issued by an individual designated by the United States department of state as a notarizing officer for performing notarial acts overseas and

attached to the record with respect to which the notarial act is performed conclusively establishes that the signature of the notarial officer is genuine and that the officer holds the indicated office.

[2017 c 281 § 14.]

### RCW 42.45.130 Certificate of notarial act.

(1) A notarial act must be evidenced by a certificate. The certificate must:

(a) Be executed contemporaneously with the performance of the notarial act;

(b) Be signed and dated by the notarial officer and, if the notarial officer is a notary public, be signed in the same manner as on file with the department;

(c) Identify the jurisdiction in which the notarial act is performed;

(d) Contain the title of office of the notarial officer;

(e) Be written in English or in dual languages, one of which must be English;

(f) If the notarial officer is a notary public, indicate the date of expiration, if any, of the officer's commission; and

(g) If the notarial act is performed under RCW 42.45.280, indicate that the notarial act was performed using communication technology.

(2) Regarding notarial act certificates on a tangible record:

(a) If a notarial act regarding a tangible record is performed by a notary public, an official stamp must be affixed to or embossed on the certificate.

(b) If a notarial act regarding a tangible record is performed by a notarial officer other than a notary public and the certificate contains the information specified in subsection (1)(b), (c), and (d) of this section, an official stamp may be affixed to or embossed on the certificate.

(3) Regarding notarial act certificates on an electronic record:

(a) If a notarial act regarding an electronic record is performed by an electronic records notary public, an official stamp must be attached to or logically associated with the certificate.

(b) If a notarial act regarding an electronic record is performed by a notarial officer other than a notary public and the certificate contains the information specified in subsection (1)(b), (c), and (d) of this section, an official stamp may be attached to or logically associated with the certificate.

(4) A certificate of a notarial act is sufficient if it meets the requirements of subsections (1) through (3) of this section and:

(a) Is in a short form set forth in RCW 42.45.140;

(b) Is in a form otherwise permitted by the law of this state;

(c) Is in a form permitted by the law applicable in the jurisdiction in which the notarial act was performed; or

(d) Sets forth the actions of the notarial officer and the actions are sufficient to meet the requirements of the notarial act as provided in RCW 42.45.030, 42.45.040, and 42.45.050 or law of this state other than this chapter.

(5) By executing a certificate of a notarial act, a notarial officer certifies that the officer has complied with the requirements and made the determinations specified in RCW 42.45.030, 42.45.040, and 42.45.050.

(6) A notarial officer may not affix the officer's signature to, or logically associate it with, a certificate until the notarial act has been performed.

(7) If a notarial act is performed regarding a tangible record, a certificate must be part of, or securely attached to, the record. If a notarial act is performed regarding an electronic record, the certificate must be affixed to, or logically associated with, the electronic record. If the director has established standards pursuant to RCW 42.45.250 for attaching, affixing, or logically associating the certificate, the process must conform to the standards.

[2019 c 154 § 4; 2017 c 281 § 15.]

NOTES:

Effective date—2019 c 154: See note following RCW 42.45.280.

### RCW 42.45.140 Short form certificates

The following short form certificates of notarial acts are sufficient for the purposes indicated, if completed with the information required by RCW 42.45.130 (1) through (4) and 42.45.280:

(1) For an acknowledgment in an individual capacity:

    State of .......
    County of .......

    This record was acknowledged before me on (date) by (name(s) of individuals).

    . . . .
    (Signature of notary public)                    (Stamp)
    . . . . (Title of office)
    My commission expires:. . . . (date)

(2) For an acknowledgment in a representative capacity:

    State of .......
    County of .......

    This record was acknowledged before me on (date) by (name(s) of individuals) as (type of authority, such as officer or trustee) of (name of party on behalf of whom record was executed).

    . . . .
    (Signature of notary public)                    (Stamp)
    . . . . (Title of office)
    My commission expires: . . . . (date)

(3) For verification on oath or affirmation:

    State of .......
    County of .......

    Signed and sworn to (or affirmed) before me on (date) by (name(s) of individuals making statement).

....
(Signature of notary public)  (Stamp)
.... (Title of office)
My commission expires: .... (date)

(4) For witnessing or attesting a signature:

State of .......
County of .......

Signed or attested before me on (date) by (name(s) of individuals).

....
(Signature of notary public)  (Stamp)
.... (Title of office)
My commission expires:. ... (date)

(5) For certifying or attesting a copy of a record:

State of .......
County of .......

I certify that this is a true and correct copy of a record in the possession of ........
Dated: ....

....
(Signature of notary public)  (Stamp)
.... (Title of office)
My commission expires: .... (date)

(6) For certifying the occurrence of an event or the performance of any act:

State of .......
County of .......

I certify that the event described in this document has occurred or been performed. Dated: ....

....
(Signature of notary public)  (Stamp)
.... (Title of office)
My commission expires: .... (date)

[2019 c 154 § 5; 2017 c 281 § 16.]

NOTES:

Effective date—2019 c 154: See note following RCW 42.45.280.

### RCW 42.45.150 Official stamp

(1) It is unlawful for any person intentionally to manufacture, give, sell, procure, or possess a seal or stamp evidencing the current appointment of a person as a notary public until the director has issued a notary commission. The official seal or stamp of

a notary public must include:

(a) The words "notary public";

(b) The words "state of Washington";

(c) The notary public's name as commissioned;

(d) The notary public's commission expiration date; and

(e) Any other information required by the director.

(2) The size and form or forms of the seal or stamp shall be prescribed by the director in rule.

(3) The seal or stamp must be capable of being copied together with the record to which it is affixed or attached or with which it is logically associated.

(4) The seal or stamp used at the time that a notarial act is performed must be the seal or stamp evidencing the notary public's commission in effect as of such time, even if the notary public has received the seal or stamp evidencing his or her next commission.

[2017 c 281 § 17.]

### RCW 42.45.160 Stamping device—Security

(1) A notary public is responsible for the security of the notary public's stamping device and may not allow another individual to use the device to perform a notarial act. On resignation from, or the revocation or expiration of, the notary public's commission, or on the expiration of the date set forth in the stamping device, the notary public shall disable the stamping device by destroying, defacing, damaging, erasing, or securing it against use in a manner that renders it unusable. On the death or adjudication of incompetency of a notary public, the notary public's personal representative or guardian or any other person knowingly in possession of the stamping device shall render it unusable by destroying, defacing, damaging, erasing, or securing it against use in a manner that renders it unusable.

(2) The seal or stamp should be kept in a locked and secured area, under the direct and exclusive control of the notary public. If a notary public's stamping device is lost or stolen, the notary public or the notary public's personal representative or guardian shall notify promptly the department on discovering that the device is lost or stolen. Any replacement device must contain a variance from the lost or stolen seal or stamp.

[2017 c 281 § 18.]

### RCW 42.45.170 Fees

(1) The director may establish by rule the maximum fees that may be charged by notaries public for various notarial services.

(2) A notary public need not charge fees for notarial acts.

[2017 c 281 § 19.]

### RCW 42.45.180 Journal

(1) A notary public shall maintain a journal in which the notary public chronicles all notarial acts that the notary public performs. The notary public shall retain the journal for ten years after the performance of the last notarial act chronicled in the journal. The journal is to be destroyed as required by the director in rule upon completion of the ten-year period.

(2) Notwithstanding any other provision of this chapter requiring a notary public to maintain a journal, a notary public who is an attorney licensed to practice law in this state is not required to chronicle a notarial act in a journal if documentation of the notarial act is otherwise maintained by professional practice.

(3) A notary public shall maintain only one tangible journal at a time to chronicle notarial acts, whether those notarial acts are performed regarding tangible or electronic records. The journal must be a permanent, bound register with numbered pages. An electronic records notary public may also maintain an electronic format journal, which can be kept concurrently with the tangible journal. The electronic journal must be in a permanent, tamper-evident electronic format complying with the rules of the director.

(4) An entry in a journal must be made contemporaneously with performance of the notarial act and contain the following information:

(a) The date and time of the notarial act;

(b) A description of the record, if any, and type of notarial act;

(c) The full name and address of each individual for whom the notarial act is performed; and

(d) Any additional information as required by the director in rule.

(5) The journal shall be kept in a locked and secured area, under the direct and exclusive control of the notary public. Failure to secure the journal may be cause for the director to take administrative action against the commission held by the notary public. If a notary public's journal is lost or stolen, the notary public promptly shall notify the department on discovering that the journal is lost or stolen.

(6) On resignation from, or the revocation or suspension of, a notary public's commission, the notary public shall retain the notary public's journal in accordance with subsection (1) of this section and inform the department where the journal is located.

[2017 c 281 § 20.]

### RCW 42.45.190 Notarial acts on electronic records—Technology—Notification—Standards

(1) A notary public may not perform notarial acts with respect to electronic records unless the notary public holds a commission as an electronic records notary public.

(2) An electronic records notary public may select one or more tamper-evident technologies to perform notarial acts with respect to electronic records that meet the standards provided in subsection (4) of this section. A person cannot require an electronic records notary public to perform a notarial act with respect to an electronic record with a technology that the notary public has not selected.

(3) Before an electronic records notary public performs the notary public's initial notarial act with respect to an electronic record, an electronic records notary public shall notify the department that he or she will be performing notarial acts with respect to electronic records and identify the technology the electronic records notary public intends to use.

(4) The director shall establish standards for approval of technology in rule. If the technology conforms to the standards, the director shall approve the use of the technology.

[2017 c 281 § 21.]

**RCW 42.45.200 Commission—Qualifications—Oath—Surety bond—Commission term—Electronic records notary public**

(1) An individual qualified under subsection (2) of this section may apply to the director for a commission as a notary public. The applicant shall comply with and provide the information required by rules established by the director and pay any application fee.

(2) An applicant for a commission as a notary public must:

(a) Be at least eighteen years of age;

(b) Be a citizen or permanent legal resident of the United States;

(c) Be a resident of or have a place of employment or practice in this state;

(d) Be able to read and write English; and

(e) Not be disqualified to receive a commission under RCW 42.45.210.

(3) Before issuance of a commission as a notary public, an applicant for the commission shall execute an oath of office and submit it to the department in the format prescribed by the director in rule.

(4) Before issuance of a commission as a notary public, the applicant for a commission shall submit to the director an assurance in the form of a surety bond in the amount established by the director in rule. The assurance must be issued by a surety or other entity licensed or authorized to write surety bonds in this state. The assurance must be effective for a four-year term or for a term that expires on the date the notary public's commission expires. The assurance must cover acts performed during the term of the notary public's commission and must be in the form prescribed by the director. If a notary public violates law with respect to notaries public in this state, the surety or issuing entity is liable under the assurance. The surety or issuing entity shall give at least thirty days' notice to the department before canceling the assurance. The surety or issuing entity shall notify the department not later than thirty days after making a payment to a claimant under the assurance. A notary public may perform notarial acts in this state only during the period that a valid assurance is on file with the department.

(5) On compliance with this section, the director shall issue a commission as a notary public to an applicant for a term of four years or for a term that expires on the date of expiration of the assurance, whichever comes first.

(6) A commission to act as a notary public authorizes the notary public to perform notarial acts. The commission does not provide the notary public any immunity or benefit conferred by law of this state on public officials or employees.

(7) An individual qualified under (a) of this subsection may apply to the director for a commission as an electronic records notary public. The applicant shall comply with and provide the information required by rules established by the director and pay the relevant application fee.

(a) An applicant for a commission as an electronic records notary public must hold a commission as notary public.

(b) An electronic records notary public commission may take the form of an endorsement to the notary public commission if deemed appropriate by the director.

[2017 c 281 § 22.]

**RCW 42.45.210 Grounds to deny, refuse to renew, revoke, suspend, or condition commission of notary public**

(1) In addition to conduct defined as unprofessional under RCW 18.235.130, the director may take action as provided for in RCW 18.235.110 against a commission as notary public for any act or omission that demonstrates the individual lacks the honesty, integrity, competence, or reliability to act as a notary public, including:

(a) Failure to comply with this chapter;

(b) A fraudulent, dishonest, or deceitful misstatement or omission in the application for a commission as a notary public submitted to the department;

(c) A conviction of the applicant or notary public of any felony or crime involving fraud, dishonesty, or deceit;

(d) A finding against, or admission of liability by, the applicant or notary public in any legal proceeding or disciplinary action based on the applicant's or notary public's fraud, dishonesty, or deceit;

(e) Failure by the notary public to discharge any duty required of a notary public, whether by this chapter, rules of the director, or any federal or state law;

(f) Use of false or misleading advertising or representation by the notary public representing that the notary public has a duty, right, or privilege that the notary public does not have;

(g) Violation by the notary public of a rule of the director regarding a notary public;

(h) Denial, refusal to renew, revocation, suspension, or conditioning of a notary public commission in another state;

(i) Failure of the notary public to maintain an assurance as provided in RCW 42.45.200(4); or

(j) Making or noting a protest of a negotiable instrument without being a person authorized by RCW 42.45.030(5).

(2) If the director denies, refuses to renew, revokes, suspends, imposes conditions, or otherwise sanctions, a commission as a notary public, the applicant or notary public is entitled to timely notice and hearing in accordance with chapter 34.05 RCW.

(3) The authority of the director to take disciplinary action on a commission as a notary public does not prevent a person from seeking and obtaining other criminal or civil remedies provided by law.

[2017 c 281 § 23.]

### RCW 42.45.220 Database of notaries public

The director shall maintain an electronic database of notaries public:

(1) Through which a person may verify the authority of a notary public to perform notarial acts; and

(2) Which indicates whether a notary public has notified the director that the notary public will be performing notarial acts on electronic records.

[2017 c 281 § 24.]

### RCW 42.45.230 Prohibited acts

(1) A commission as a notary public does not authorize an individual to:

(a) Assist persons in drafting legal records, give legal advice, or otherwise practice law;

(b) Act as an immigration consultant or an expert on immigration matters;

(c) Represent a person in a judicial or administrative proceeding relating to immigration to the United States, United States citizenship, or related matters;

(d) Receive compensation for performing any of the activities listed in this subsection; or

(e) Provide court reporting services.

(2) A notary public may not engage in false or deceptive advertising.

(3) A notary public, other than an attorney licensed to practice law in this state, or a Washington-licensed limited license legal technician acting within the scope of his or her license, may not use the term "notario" or "notario publico."

(4) A notary public, other than an attorney licensed to practice law in this state or a limited license legal technician acting within the scope of his or her license, may not assist another person in selecting the appropriate certificate required by RCW 42.45.130.

(5) A notary public, other than an attorney licensed to practice law in this state, or a Washington-licensed limited license legal technician acting within the scope of his or her license, may not advertise or represent that the notary public may assist persons in drafting legal records, give legal advice, or otherwise practice law. If a notary public who is not an attorney licensed to practice law in this state, or a Washington-licensed limited license legal technician acting within the scope of his or her license, in any manner advertises or represents that the notary public offers notarial services, whether orally or in a record, including broadcast media, print media, and the internet, the notary public shall include the following statement, or an alternate statement authorized or required by the director, in the advertisement or representation, prominently and in each language used in the advertisement or representation: "I am not an attorney licensed to practice law in this state. I am not allowed to draft legal records, give advice on legal matters, including immigration, or charge a fee for those activities." If the form of advertisement or representation is not broadcast media, print media, or the internet and does not permit inclusion of the statement required by this subsection because of size, it must be displayed prominently or provided at the place of performance of the notarial act before the notarial act is performed.

(6) Except as otherwise allowed by law, a notary public may not withhold access to or possession of an original record provided by a person that seeks performance of a notarial act by the notary public. A notary public may not maintain copies or electronic images of documents notarized unless the copies or images are maintained by an attorney or Washington-licensed limited license legal technician acting within his or her scope of practice for the performance of legal services or for other services performed for the client and the copies or images are not maintained solely as part of the notary transaction.

[2017 c 281 § 25.]

### RCW 42.45.240 Validity of notarial acts

Except as otherwise provided in RCW 42.45.020(2), the failure of a notarial officer to perform a duty or meet a requirement specified in this chapter does not invalidate a notarial act performed by the notarial officer. The validity of a notarial act under this chapter does not prevent an aggrieved person from seeking to invalidate the record or transaction that is the subject of the notarial act or from seeking other remedies based on law of this state other than this chapter or law of the United States. This section does not validate a purported notarial act performed by an individual who does not have the authority to perform notarial acts. Nothing in chapter 281, Laws of

2017 gives the director authority to invalidate a notarial act.

[2017 c 281 § 26.]

### RCW 42.45.250 Rules

(1) The director may adopt rules necessary to implement this chapter.

(2) In adopting, amending, or repealing rules about notarial acts with respect to electronic records, the director shall consider standards, practices, and customs of other jurisdictions that substantially enact this chapter.

[2017 c 281 § 27.]

### RCW 42.45.260 Commissions in effect July 1, 2018—Continuation

A commission as a notary public in effect on July 1, 2018, continues until its date of expiration. A notary public who applies to renew a commission as a notary public on or after July 1, 2018, is subject to and shall comply with this chapter. A notary public, in performing notarial acts after July 1, 2018, shall comply with this chapter.

[2017 c 281 § 28.]

### RCW 42.45.270 Uniform regulation of business and professions act—Application

The uniform regulation of business and professions act, chapter 18.235 RCW, governs unlicensed practice, the issuance and denial of licenses, and the discipline of licensees under this chapter.

[2017 c 281 § 32.]

### RCW 42.45.280 Electronic records notary public

(1) The definitions in this subsection apply throughout this section unless the context clearly requires otherwise.

(a) "Communication technology" means an electronic device or process that:

(i) Allows an electronic records notary public and a remotely located individual to communicate with each other simultaneously by sight and sound; and

(ii) When necessary under and consistent with other applicable law, facilitates communication with a remotely located individual with a vision, hearing, or speech impairment.

(b) "Foreign state" means a jurisdiction other than the United States, a state, or a federally recognized Indian tribe.

(c) "Identity proofing" means a process or service by which a third person provides an electronic records notary public with a means to verify the identity of a remotely located individual by a review of personal information from public or private data sources.

(d) "Outside the United States" means a location outside the geographic boundaries of the United States, Puerto Rico, the United States Virgin Islands, and any territory, insular possession, or other location subject to the jurisdiction of the United States.

(e) "Remotely located individual" means an individual who is not in the physical presence of the electronic records notary public who performs a notarial act under subsection (3) of this section.

(2) A remotely located individual complies with RCW 42.45.040 by using communication technology to appear before an electronic records notary public.

(3) An electronic records notary public located in this state may perform a notarial act using communication technology for a remotely located individual if:

(a) The electronic records notary public:

(i) Has personal knowledge under RCW 42.45.050(1) of the identity of the remotely located individual;

(ii) Has satisfactory evidence of the identity of the remotely located individual by a verification on oath or affirmation of a credible witness appearing before and identified by the electronic records notary public under RCW 42.45.050(2); or

(iii) Has obtained satisfactory evidence of the identity of the remotely located individual by using at least two different types of identity proofing;

(b) The electronic records notary public is reasonably able to confirm that a record before the electronic records notary public is the same record in which the remotely located individual made a statement or on which the individual executed a signature;

(c) The electronic records notary public, or a person acting on behalf of the electronic records notary public, creates an audio-visual recording of the performance of the notarial act; and

(d) For a remotely located individual located outside the United States:

(i) The record:

(A) Is to be filed with or relates to a matter before a public official or court, governmental entity, or other entity subject to the jurisdiction of the United States; or

(B) Involves property located in the territorial jurisdiction of the United States or involves a transaction substantially connected with the United States; and

(ii) The act of making the statement or signing the record is not prohibited by the foreign state in which the remotely located individual is located.

(4) If a notarial act is performed under this section, the certificate of notarial act required by RCW 42.45.130 and the short form certificate provided in RCW 42.45.140 must indicate that the notarial act was performed using communication technology.

(5) A short form certificate provided in RCW 42.45.140 for a notarial act subject to this section is sufficient if it:

(a) Complies with rules adopted under subsection (8)(a) of this section; or

(b) Is in the form provided by RCW 42.45.140 and contains a statement substantially as follows: "This notarial act involved the use of communication technology."

(6) An electronic records notary public, a guardian, conservator, or agent of an electronic records notary public, or a personal representative of a deceased electronic records notary public shall retain the audio-visual recording created under subsection (3)(c) of this section or cause the recording to be retained by a repository designated by or on behalf of the person required to retain the recording. Unless a different period is required by rule adopted under subsection (8)(d) of this section, the recording must be retained for a period of at least ten years after the recording is made.

(7) Before an electronic records notary public performs the electronic records notary public's initial notarial act under this section, the electronic records notary public must notify the director that the electronic records notary public will be performing notarial acts and identify the technologies the electronic records notary public intends to use.

If the director has established standards under subsection (8) of this section and RCW 42.45.250 for approval of communication technology or identity proofing, the communication technology and identity proofing must conform to the standards.

(8) In addition to adopting rules under RCW 42.45.250, the director may adopt rules under this section regarding performance of a notarial act. The rules may:

(a) Prescribe the means of performing a notarial act involving a remotely located individual using communication technology;

(b) Establish standards for communication technology and identity proofing;

(c) Establish requirements or procedures to approve providers of communication technology and the process of identity proofing; and

(d) Establish standards and a period for the retention of an audio-visual recording created under subsection (3)(c) of this section.

(9) Before adopting, amending, or repealing a rule governing performance of a notarial act with respect to a remotely located individual, the director must consider:

(a) The most recent standards regarding the performance of a notarial act with respect to a remotely located individual adopted by national standard-setting organizations and the recommendations of the national association of secretaries of state;

(b) Standards, practices, and customs of other jurisdictions that have laws substantially similar to this section; and

(c) The views of governmental officials and entities and other interested persons.

[2019 c 154 § 1.]

NOTES:

Effective date—2019 c 154: "This act takes effect October 1, 2020." [ 2019 c 154 § 10.]

### RCW 42.45.900 Short title

This chapter may be known and cited as the 2018 revised uniform law on notarial acts.

[2019 c 154 § 6; 2017 c 281 § 1.]

NOTES:

Effective date—2019 c 154: See note following RCW 42.45.280.

### RCW 42.45.901 Application

This chapter applies to a notarial act performed on or after July 1, 2018.

[2017 c 281 § 3.]

### RCW 42.45.902 Savings This chapter does not affect the validity or effect of a notarial act performed before July 1, 2018.

[2017 c 281 § 29.]

### RCW 42.45.903 Application—Construction

In applying and construing this uniform act, consideration must be given to the need to promote uniformity of the law with respect to its subject matter among states that enact it.

[2017 c 281 § 30.]

**RCW 42.45.904 Relation to electronic signatures in global and national commerce act**

This chapter modifies, limits, and supersedes the electronic signatures in global and national commerce act, 15 U.S.C. Sec. 7001 et seq., but does not modify, limit, or supersede section 101(c) of that act, 15 U.S.C. Sec. 7001(c), or authorize electronic delivery of any of the notices described in section 103(b) of that act, 15 U.S.C. Sec. 7003(b).

[2017 c 281 § 31.]

**RCW 42.45.905**

Effective date—2017 c 281.

This act takes effect July 1, 2018.

[2017 c 281 § 44.]

## WASHINGTON ADMINISTRATIVE CODE

### Title 308. Licensing, Department of
### Chapter 30. Notaries Public

**WAC Sections**

| | |
|---|---|
| 308-30-010 | Authority. |
| 308-30-020 | Definitions. |
| 308-30-030 | Application process for notary public commission. |
| 308-30-040 | Approval or denial of application. |
| 308-30-050 | Term of commission. |
| 308-30-060 | Application fees. |
| 308-30-070 | Size and form of official seal or stamp. |
| 308-30-080 | Acquiring official seal or stamp. |
| 308-30-090 | Replacement of lost or stolen official seal or stamp. |
| 308-30-100 | Notary signature. |
| 308-30-110 | Requirements for notarial acts. |
| 308-30-120 | Authorized electronic notarial acts. |
| 308-30-130 | Requirements for technologies and technology providers. |
| 308-30-140 | Refusal of requests to use system. |
| 308-30-150 | Completion of electronic notarial certificate. |
| 308-30-160 | Certification of electronic notarial acts. |
| 308-30-170 | Electronic notarial signature. |
| 308-30-180 | Electronic notarial stamp. |
| 308-30-190 | Journal of notarial acts required. |
| 308-30-200 | Format of journals of notarial acts. |
| 308-30-210 | Disposition of journal. |

| | |
|---|---|
| 308-30-220 | Fees for notarial acts. |
| 308-30-230 | Testimonials. |
| 308-30-240 | Forms. |
| 308-30-250 | Change of name or address. |
| 308-30-260 | Evidence of authenticity. |
| 308-30-270 | Termination or suspension of commission or endorsement. |
| 308-30-280 | Change of application information. |
| 308-30-290 | Authorized remote notarial acts. |
| 308-30-300 | Standards for identity proofing. |
| 308-30-310 | Standards for communication technology. |
| 308-30-320 | Certificate of notarial act for remote notarial acts. |
| 308-30-330 | Retention of audio-visual recordings and repositories. |

### 308-30-010 - Authority

This chapter implements the revised uniform law on notarial acts, chapter 42.45 RCW.

[Statutory Authority: RCW 42.45.250. WSR 18-12-028, § 308-30-010, filed 5/29/18, effective 7/1/18. Statutory Authority: RCW 42.44.190. WSR 93-05-009, § 308-30-010, filed 2/5/93, effective 3/8/93. Statutory Authority: 1985 c 156 §§ 5 and 20. WSR 85-24-025 (Order PL 571), § 308-30-010, filed 11/26/85, effective 1/1/86.]

### 308-30-020 - Definitions

Words and terms used in these rules have the same meaning as in the Revised Uniform Law on Notarial Acts, RCW 42.45.010.

"Appear personally" means:

(a) Being in the same physical location as another individual and close enough to see, hear, communicate with, and exchange tangible identification credentials with that individual; or

(b) For remote notarial acts, being in a different physical location from another individual but able to see, hear, and communicate with that individual by means of communication technology.

"Commission" is equivalent to the term "license" as defined in RCW 18.235.010(6).

"Department" means the Washington state department of licensing.

"Director" means the director of the department of licensing or the director's designee.

"Electronic journal" means a chronological record of notarizations maintained by a notary public in an electronic format in compliance with these rules.

"Electronic notarial acts" means notarizations or notarial acts with respect to electronic records.

"Electronic notarial certificate" means the part of, or attachment to, an electronic record that is completed by the notary public, contains the information required under RCW 42.45.130 and the notary's official stamp, bears that notary's electronic signature, and states the facts attested to by the notary in a notarization performed on an electronic record.

"Enroll" and "enrollment" mean a process for registering a notary public with a technology provider to access and use a tamper-evident technology in order to perform electronic notarial acts.

"Principal" means:

(a) An individual whose electronic signature is notarized; or

(b) An individual, other than a witness required for an electronic notarial act, taking an oath or affirmation from the notary public.

"Remote notarial act" means a notarization that is performed using audio-video technology that meets the requirements in WAC 308-30-310 that allows for direct interaction between the notary and the individuals that are remotely located.

"Sole control" means at all times being in the direct physical custody of the notary public or safeguarded by the notary with a password or other secure means of authentication.

"Tamper-evident technology" means a set of applications, programs, hardware, software, or other technologies designed to enable a notary public to perform electronic notarial acts and to display evidence of any changes made to an electronic record.

"Technology provider" means an individual or entity that offers the services of a tamper-evident technology for electronic notarial acts.

"Venue" means the state and county where the notary public is physically located while performing a notarial act.

[Statutory Authority: RCW 42.45.250. WSR 21-05-039, § 308-30-020, filed 2/11/21, effective 3/14/21; WSR 18-12-028, § 308-30-020, filed 5/29/18, effective 7/1/18. Statutory Authority: RCW 42.44.190. WSR 06-20-061, § 308-30-020, filed 9/29/06, effective 11/1/06; WSR 93-05-009, § 308-30-020, filed 2/5/93, effective 3/8/93. Statutory Authority: 1985 c 156 §§ 5 and 20. WSR 85-24-025 (Order PL 571), § 308-30-020, filed 11/26/85, effective 1/1/86.]

### 308-30-030 - Application process for notary public commission

(1) To apply for a notary public commission, an applicant who meets the requirements of RCW 42.45.200(2) shall submit an application on forms provided by the department. The application shall include:

(a) Evidence of a ten thousand dollar surety bond, signed by the notary public, that conforms to RCW 42.45.200(4);

(b) Payment of the prescribed fee; and

(c) A signed and notarized oath of office.

(2) As part of a notary public commission application, an applicant shall provide both their legal name and their commission name. The applicant's commission name must contain their surname, and at least the initials of the applicant's first and middle name.

(3) To apply for an electronic records notary public endorsement, an applicant who meets the requirements of RCW 42.45.200(7) shall submit an electronic records notary public application on forms provided by the department and pay the prescribed fee.

(4) An applicant may only apply for an electronic records notary public endorsement if:

(a) They currently hold an active notary public commission; or

(b) They are applying for a notary public commission and an electronic records notary public endorsement simultaneously.

(5) An individual applying for an electronic records notary public endorsement must inform the department within thirty days of applying of the tamper-evident technology provider that they have enrolled with before they perform their first electronic notarial act.

(6) To apply for a remote notary endorsement, an electronic records notary public shall submit a remote notary endorsement application on forms provided by the department.

(7) An applicant may only apply for a remote notary endorsement if:

(a) They currently hold an active notary public commission with an electronic records notary public endorsement;

(b) They currently hold an active notary public commission, and are applying for an electronic records notary public endorsement and a remote notary endorsement simultaneously; or

(c) They are applying for a notary public commission, an electronic records notary public endorsement, and a remote notarial acts endorsement simultaneously.

(8) A notary public shall reapply with the department for each commission term before performing notarial acts.

(9) A notary public may elect not to apply for an electronic records notary public endorsement or a remote notary endorsement.

[Statutory Authority: RCW 42.45.250. WSR 21-05-039, § 308-30-030, filed 2/11/21, effective 3/14/21; WSR 18-12-028, § 308-30-030, filed 5/29/18, effective 7/1/18. Statutory Authority: RCW 42.44.190. WSR 93-05-009, § 308-30-030, filed 2/5/93, effective 3/8/93. Statutory Authority: 1985 c 156 §§ 5 and 20. WSR 85-24-025 (Order PL 571), § 308-30-030, filed 11/26/85, effective 1/1/86.]

### 308-30-040 - Approval or denial of application

(1) Upon an applicant's fulfillment of the requirements for a notary public commission and/or an electronic records notary public endorsement, and/or a remote notary endorsement, the department shall approve the application and issue the notary public commission and/or any appropriate endorsements.

(2) If the department receives an incomplete or invalid application, the department shall hold the application for thirty calendar days to allow the applicant to cure any defects. After the thirty day period, the application shall be canceled and any application fees forfeited.

(3) An applicant may not perform any notarial acts on a tangible or electronic record before receiving a notary public commission and the appropriate endorsement from the department.

(4) The department may deny a commission or endorsement application if the applicant fails to comply with these rules or does not meet the requirements for licensure.

[Statutory Authority: RCW 42.45.250. WSR 21-05-039, § 308-30-040, filed 2/11/21, effective 3/14/21; WSR 18-12-028, § 308-30-040, filed 5/29/18, effective 7/1/18. Statutory Authority: RCW 42.44.190. WSR 93-05-009, § 308-30-040, filed 2/5/93, effective 3/8/93. Statutory Authority: 1985 c 156 §§ 5 and 20. WSR 85-24-025 (Order PL 571), § 308-30-040, filed 11/26/85, effective 1/1/86.]

### 308-30-050 - Term of commission

(1) The term of a notary public commission shall expire on the expiration date of the notary public's surety bond, no more than four years after their commission date.

(2) Unless terminated pursuant to WAC 308-30-270, an electronic records notary public endorsement and the remote notary endorsement are valid from the date the endorsement is issued by the department, and continues as long as the notary public's current commission remains valid.

[Statutory Authority: RCW 42.45.250. WSR 21-05-039, § 308-30-050, filed 2/11/21, effective 3/14/21; WSR 18-12-028, § 308-30-050, filed 5/29/18, effective 7/1/18. Statutory Authority: RCW 42.44.190. WSR 93-05-009, § 308-30-050, filed 2/5/93, effective 3/8/93. Statutory Authority: 1985 c 156 §§ 5 and 20. WSR 85-24-025 (Order PL 571), § 308-30-050, filed 11/26/85, effective 1/1/86.]

### 308-30-060 - Application fees

The following fees shall be charged by the department:

| Title of Fee | Fee |
|---|---|
| Application for notary public commission | $30.00 |
| Application for electronic records notary public endorsement | $15.00 |
| Renewal of notary public commission | $30.00 |
| Renewal of electronic records notary public endorsement | $15.00 |
| Duplicate certificate of commission (including name change) | $15.00 |

[Statutory Authority: RCW 42.45.250. WSR 18-12-028, § 308-30-060, filed 5/29/18, effective 7/1/18. Statutory Authority: RCW 42.44.190. WSR 93-05-009, § 308-30-060, filed 2/5/93, effective 3/8/93. Statutory Authority: 1985 c 156 §§ 5 and 20. WSR 85-24-025 (Order PL 571), § 308-30-060, filed 11/26/85, effective 1/1/86.]

### 308-30-070 - Size and form of official seal or stamp

An official seal or stamp shall conform to the following requirements:

(1) The seal or stamp shall include the following information:

(a) The words "notary public";

(b) The words "state of Washington";

(c) The notary public's name as commissioned;

(d) The notary public's commission expiration date; and

(e) The notary public's commission number.

(2) The type on this seal or stamp shall be a minimum of 8 point type.

(3) The seal or stamp shall conform to the following physical requirements:

(a) The seal or stamp shall be minimum one and five-eighths inches diameter if circular, or one inch wide by one and five-eighths inches long if rectangular;

(b) The face of the seal or stamp shall be permanently affixed; and

(c) If the stamp is affixed to a tangible record, it shall be applied in permanent ink and shall be capable of being photocopied.

(4) The seal or stamp shall not contain the Washington state seal.

[Statutory Authority: RCW 42.45.250. WSR 18-12-028, § 308-30-070, filed 5/29/18, effective 7/1/18. Statutory Authority: RCW 42.44.190. WSR 93-05-009, § 308-30-070, filed 2/5/93, effective 3/8/93. Statutory Authority: 1985 c 156 §§ 5 and 20. WSR 85-24-025 (Order PL 571), § 308-30-070, filed 11/26/85, effective 1/1/86.]

### 308-30-080 - Acquiring official seal or stamp

(1) A notary public shall procure an official seal or stamp only after receiving a certificate evidencing the notary public's commission from the department, and shall provide a copy of this certificate to their chosen seal or stamp vendor as part of procuring the stamp.

(2) A notary public with a commission in effect on July 1, 2018, may continue to use their notarial seal until the commission's date of expiration. A notary public who procures an official seal or stamp after July 1, 2018, is subject to and shall comply with the rules in WAC 308-30-070.

(3) The stamp a notary public acquires is the exclusive property of the notary public, and shall not be surrendered to an employer upon termination of employment, regardless of whether the employer paid for the seal or for the notary's bond or appointment fees.

[Statutory Authority: RCW 42.45.250. WSR 18-12-028, § 308-30-080, filed 5/29/18, effective 7/1/18. Statutory Authority: RCW 42.44.190. WSR 93-05-009, § 308-30-080, filed 2/5/93, effective 3/8/93. Statutory Authority: 1985 c 156 §§ 5 and 20. WSR 85-24-025 (Order PL 571), § 308-30-080, filed 11/26/85, effective 1/1/86.]

### 308-30-090 - Replacement of lost or stolen official seal or stamp

(1) When an official seal or stamp is lost or stolen the notary public shall notify the department in writing within ten business days of discovering the seal or stamp was lost or stolen.

(2) The notary public may not obtain a replacement official seal or stamp until they have properly notified the department that the original was lost or stolen.

(3) A replacement official seal or stamp must contain some variance from the original seal or stamp.

(4) If the lost or stolen official seal or stamp is found or recovered after a replacement has been obtained, the original seal or stamp shall be destroyed.

[Statutory Authority: RCW 42.45.250. WSR 18-12-028, § 308-30-090, filed 5/29/18, effective 7/1/18. Statutory Authority: RCW 42.44.190. WSR 93-05-009, § 308-30-090, filed 2/5/93, effective 3/8/93. Statutory Authority: 1985 c 156 §§ 5 and 20. WSR 85-24-025 (Order PL 571), § 308-30-090, filed 11/26/85, effective 1/1/86.]

### 308-30-100 - Notary signature.

In addition to the requirements listed in RCW 42.45.130, a notary public signing the notarial certificate of a completed notarial act shall sign the notarial certificate using the exact name that appears on the notary's certificate of commission and their seal or stamp.

[Statutory Authority: RCW 42.45.250. WSR 18-12-028, § 308-30-100, filed 5/29/18, effective 7/1/18. Statutory Authority: RCW 42.44.190, 43.35.055, 43.24.086, WAC 308-30-100. WSR 05-12-047, § 308-30-100, filed 5/26/05, effective 6/26/05. Statutory Authority: RCW 43.24.086. WSR 90-06-052, § 308-30-100, filed 3/2/90, effective 4/2/90. Statutory Authority: 1985 c 156 §§ 5 and 20. WSR 85-24-025 (Order PL 571), § 308-30-100, filed 11/26/85, effective 1/1/86.]

### 308-30-110 - Requirements for notarial acts

(1) In performing a notarial act, the notary public shall be physically within the geographic borders of the state of Washington.

(2) A notarial officer who certifies that an event has occurred or an act has been performed shall determine, from personal knowledge or satisfactory evidence, that the occurrence or performance took place.

(3) Electronic notarial acts shall conform to the requirements listed in these rules and RCW 42.45.040 on signing parties appearing before the notary.

[Statutory Authority: RCW 42.45.250. WSR 18-12-028, § 308-30-110, filed 5/29/18, effective 7/1/18.]

### 308-30-120 - Authorized electronic notarial acts

A notary public who has received an electronic records notary public endorsement from the department may perform the following electronic notarial acts:

(1) Taking an acknowledgment;

(2) Taking a verification on oath or affirmation;

(3) Witnessing or attesting a signature;

(4) Certifying or attesting a copy;

(5) Certifying that an event has occurred or an act has been performed; and

(6) Noting a protest of a negotiable instrument, if the notary public is:

(a) Licensed to practice law in the state of Washington;

(b) Acting under the authority of an attorney who is licensed to practice law in this or another state; or

(c) Acting under the authority of a financial institution regulated by this state, another state, or the federal government.

[Statutory Authority: RCW 42.45.250. WSR 18-12-028, § 308-30-120, filed 5/29/18, effective 7/1/18. Statutory Authority: RCW 42.44.190. WSR 93-05-009, § 308-30-120, filed 2/5/93, effective 3/8/93.]

### 308-30-130 - Requirements for technologies and technology providers

A tamper-evident technology shall comply with these rules:

(1) A technology provider shall enroll only notaries public who have been issued an electronic records notary public endorsement pursuant to WAC 308-30-030.

(2) A technology provider shall take reasonable steps to ensure that a notary public who has enrolled to use the technology has the knowledge to use it to perform electronic notarial acts in compliance with these rules.

(3) A tamper-evident technology shall require access to the system by a password or other secure means of authentication.

(4) A tamper-evident technology shall enable a notary public to affix the notary's electronic signature and seal or stamp in a manner that attributes such signature and seal or stamp to the notary.

(5) A technology provider shall provide prorated fees to align the usage and cost of the tamper-evident technology with the term limit of the notary public electronic records notary public endorsement.

(6) A technology provider shall suspend the use of any tamper-evident technology for any notary public whose endorsement has been revoked, suspended, or canceled by the state of Washington or the notary public.

[Statutory Authority: RCW 42.45.250. WSR 18-12-028, § 308-30-130, filed 5/29/18, effective 7/1/18. Statutory Authority: RCW 42.44.190. WSR 93-05-009, § 308-30-130, filed 2/5/93, effective 3/8/93.]

### 308-30-140 - Refusal of requests to use system

In addition to the reasons listed in RCW 42.45.060, a notary public shall refuse a request to:

(1) Use a tamper-evident technology that the notary does not know how to operate; or

(2) Perform an electronic notarial act if the notary has a reasonable belief that a tamper-evident technology does not meet the requirements set forth in these rules.

[Statutory Authority: RCW 42.45.250. WSR 18-12-028, § 308-30-140, filed 5/29/18, effective 7/1/18. Statutory Authority: RCW 42.44.190. WSR 93-05-009, § 308-30-140, filed 2/5/93, effective 3/8/93.]

### 308-30-150 - Completion of electronic notarial certificate

(1) For every electronic notarial act and remote notarial act, a notary public shall complete an electronic notarial certificate that complies with the requirements of these rules, RCW 42.45.130 and 42.45.140.

(2) An electronic notarial certificate shall be completed at the time of notarization and in the presence of the principal.

[Statutory Authority: RCW 42.45.250. WSR 21-05-039, § 308-30-150, filed 2/11/21, effective 3/14/21; WSR 18-12-028, § 308-30-150, filed 5/29/18, effective 7/1/18. Statutory Authority: RCW 42.44.190. WSR 93-05-009, § 308-30-150, filed 2/5/93, effective 3/8/93.]

### 308-30-160 - Certification of electronic notarial acts

A notary public shall sign each electronic notarial certificate with an electronic signature that complies with WAC 308-30-170 and authenticate an electronic notarial act with an official stamp that complies with WAC 380-30-180.

[Statutory Authority: RCW 42.45.250. WSR 18-12-028, § 308-30-160, filed 5/29/18, effective 7/1/18. Statutory Authority: RCW 42.44.190. WSR 93-05-009, § 308-30-160, filed 2/5/93, effective 3/8/93.]

### 308-30-170 - Electronic notarial signature

(1) A notary public shall use a tamper-evident technology that complies with WAC 308-30-130 of these rules to produce the notary's electronic signature in a manner that is capable of independent verification.

(2) A notary public shall take reasonable steps to ensure that no other individual may possess or access a tamper-evident technology used to produce the notary's electronic signature.

(3) A notary public shall keep in the sole control of the notary all or any part of a tamper-evident technology whose exclusive purpose is to perform electronic notarial acts.

(4) For the purposes of this section, "capable of independent verification" means that any interested individual may confirm through the department that a notary public who signed an electronic record in an official capacity had authority at that time to perform electronic notarial acts.

[Statutory Authority: RCW 42.45.250. WSR 18-12-028, § 308-30-170, filed 5/29/18, effective 7/1/18. Statutory Authority: RCW 34.05.410 (1)(a) and 34.05.482 (1)(c). WSR 97-10-052, § 308-30-170, filed 5/1/97, effective 6/1/97.]

### 308-30-180 - Electronic notarial stamp

(1) An electronic stamp may be used to authenticate an electronic notarial act if the electronic notarial certificate conforms to the rules set forth in RCW 42.45.130 and 42.45.140.

(2) An electronic stamp of a notary public used to authenticate an electronic notarial act shall conform to RCW 42.45.150 and WAC 308-30-070.

(3) The electronic stamp of a notary public shall be a digital image that appears in the likeness or representation of a traditional physical notary public official stamp meeting the requirements of RCW 42.45.150 and WAC 308-30-070.

(4) The tamper-evident technology used to create a notary public's electronic stamp shall not be used for any purpose other than performing electronic notarial acts under chapter 42.45 RCW and these rules.

(5) Only the notary public to whom the tamper-evident technology is registered shall generate an official stamp.

[Statutory Authority: RCW 42.45.250. WSR 18-12-028, § 308-30-180, filed 5/29/18, effective 7/1/18. Statutory Authority: RCW 34.05.410 (1)(a) and 34.05.482 (1)(c). WSR 97-10-052, § 308-30-180, filed 5/1/97, effective 6/1/97.]

### 308-30-190 - Journal of notarial acts required

(1) A notary public shall record each notarial act in a journal at the time of notarization in compliance with RCW 42.45.180 and these rules.

(2) If a notary public performs notarial acts involving different statements or documents for the same individual on the same date, the notary public may record a single entry in the journal for all of the statements or documents. The entry shall include the number of statements or documents notarized and shall otherwise conform to RCW 42.45.180 and these rules.

(3) The fact that the notary public's employer or contractor keeps a record of notarial acts shall not relieve the notary of the duties required by these rules.

[Statutory Authority: RCW 42.45.250. WSR 18-12-028, § 308-30-190, filed 5/29/18, effective 7/1/18. Statutory Authority: RCW 34.05.410 (1)(a) and 34.05.482 (1)(c). WSR 97-10-052, § 308-30-190, filed 5/1/97, effective 6/1/97.]

### 308-30-200 - Format of journals of notarial acts

(1) A tangible notarial journal shall:

(a) Be a permanent, bound book with numbered pages; and

(b) Have the capacity to record for each notarial act:

(i) The information required by RCW 42.45.180(4);

(ii) A description of the notary public's method of identifying the principal; and

(iii) The principal's signature, or the signature of an authorized party in compliance with RCW 42.45.070, or a notation in the notary journal that the notarial act was performed via remote notarization.

(2) If a notary public keeps an electronic journal pursuant to RCW 42.45.180(3), the electronic journal shall:

(a) Be maintained only in addition to the tangible journal;

(b) Have the capacity to record the information required for a tangible notarial journal;

(c) Enable access by a password or other secure means of authentication;

(d) Be tamper-evident;

(e) Create a duplicate record of the journal as a backup; and

(f) Be capable of providing tangible or electronic copies of any entry made in the journal.

(3) A notary public's journal is the exclusive property of the notary public, and shall not be surrendered to an employer upon demand or termination, whether the employer paid for the journal or the notary's bond or application fees.

(4) A notary performing remote notarization must maintain a tangible notary journal as required in RCW 42.45.180 and WAC 308-30-190, this section, and WAC 308-30-210. Notaries performing remote notarization are not required to collect and maintain the signatures of the signers when those notarizations were performed remotely. Notaries must note in their tangible notary log that a notarization was performed remotely.

[Statutory Authority: RCW 42.45.250. WSR 21-05-039, § 308-30-200, filed 2/11/21, effective 3/14/21; WSR 18-12-028, § 308-30-200, filed 5/29/18, effective 7/1/18.]

### 308-30-210 - Disposition of journal

(1) Ten years after the performance of the last notarial act chronicled in a tangible journal, the journal is to be destroyed by shredding or other destruction that leaves any entry in the journal illegible.

(2) Ten years after the performance of the last notarial act chronicled in an electronic journal, the journal is to be destroyed by deleting any remaining records pertaining to the electronic journal and deleting any remaining tamper-evident technology in the notary's possession.

(3) The personal representative or guardian of a notary public shall follow RCW 42.45.180(6) related to the disposition of the notary public's journals upon the death or adjudication of incompetency of the notary public.

(4) Nothing in this section shall require a notary to dispose of their notarial journal or journals if doing so would be in conflict with the law of another jurisdiction that requires a notary to keep their journal for a longer period of time.

(5) The notary public, or the notary's personal representative, shall provide access instructions to the department for any electronic journal maintained or stored by the notary, upon commission resignation, revocation, or expiration without renewal, or upon the death or adjudicated incompetence of the notary.

[Statutory Authority: RCW 42.45.250. WSR 18-12-028, § 308-30-210, filed 5/29/18, effective 7/1/18.]

### 308-30-220 - Fees for notarial acts

(1) The maximum fees a notary may charge for notarial acts are:

Notarial Act................................................................................................... Fee

Witnessing or attesting a signature ..................................................................................$10.00

Taking an acknowledgment or a verification upon oath or affirmation ....................$10.00

Certifying or attesting a copy.................................................................................................$10.00

Administering an oath or affirmation..................................................................................$10.00

Certifying that an event has occurred or an act has been performed .......................$10.00

(2) A notary public need not charge for notarial acts.

(3) A notary public may not charge fees for receiving or noting a protest of a negotiable instrument.

(4) A notary public may additionally charge the actual costs of copying any instrument or record.

(5) A notary public may charge a travel fee when traveling to perform a notarial act if:

(a) The notary public and the individual requesting the notarial act agree upon the travel fee in advance of the travel; and

(b) The notary public explains to the individual requesting the notarial act that the travel fee is in addition to the notarial fee in subsection (1) of this section and is not required by law.

(6) Notwithstanding the maximum fees set forth in subsection (1) of this section and the prohibition set forth in subsection (3) of this section, a notary public may charge a maximum fee of twenty-five dollars to perform a remote notarial act.

[Statutory Authority: RCW 42.45.250. WSR 21-05-039, § 308-30-220, filed 2/11/21, effective 3/14/21; WSR 18-12-028, § 308-30-220, filed 5/29/18, effective 7/1/18.]

### 308-30-230 - Testimonials

A notary may not endorse or promote any service, contest, or other offering if the notary's seal or title is used in the endorsement or promotional statement.

[Statutory Authority: RCW 42.45.250. WSR 18-12-028, § 308-30-230, filed 5/29/18, effective 7/1/18.]

### 308-30-240 - Forms

(1) The forms in RCW 42.45.140 are examples of certificates with the sufficient information included. When a specific form is required by another statute of this state, the required form shall be used.

(2) A nonattorney notary may not assist another person in drafting, completing, selecting, or understanding a document or transaction requiring a notarial act. This does not preclude a notary who is duly qualified in a particular profession from giving advice relating to matters in that professional field.

[Statutory Authority: RCW 42.45.250. WSR 18-12-028, § 308-30-240, filed 5/29/18, effective 7/1/18.]

### 308-30-250 - Change of name or address

(1) When a notary public changes his or her name or address, the department of licensing must be notified of such change on forms prescribed by the department.

(2) A name change notification must be accompanied by a bond rider from the

bonding company amending the notary bond, and the prescribed fee for a name change which provides a duplicate notary certificate showing the new name. There is no charge for an address change and a new certificate is not issued.

(3) A notary that submits a name change notification shall continue to use their original notary stamp or seal and their original name and signature until they receive a new commission certificate and seal or stamp with the new information.

[Statutory Authority: RCW 42.45.250. WSR 18-12-028, § 308-30-250, filed 5/29/18, effective 7/1/18.]

### 308-30-260 - Evidence of authenticity

Requests for evidence of authenticity should be addressed to the Washington office of the secretary of state, corporations and charities division.

[Statutory Authority: RCW 42.45.250. WSR 18-12-028, § 308-30-260, filed 5/29/18, effective 7/1/18.]

### 308-30-270 - Termination or suspension of commission or endorsement

(1) The department may take action against the commission and/or endorsement of a notary public who fails to comply with these rules as provided in RCW 42.45.210, 42.45.270, and chapter 18.235 RCW. Any restriction, suspension, or revocation of a notary public's commission will automatically have the same effect on any endorsement the notary public holds.

(2) A notary public may terminate their notary public commission and/or electronic records endorsement or remote notary endorsement by notifying the department of this intent in writing and disposing of all or any part of a tamper-evident technology in the notary's control whose purpose was to perform electronic notarizations.

(3) A notary public may terminate the electronic records notary public endorsement or the remote notary endorsement and maintain the underlying notary public commission.

(4) A notary public whose commission is terminated or expired, either by the notary or the department, shall disable their official stamp by destroying, defacing, damaging, or securing the device against use. The notary shall maintain their notarial journals for ten years as required by RCW 42.45.180 and WAC 308-30-210.

[Statutory Authority: RCW 42.45.250. WSR 21-05-039, § 308-30-270, filed 2/11/21, effective 3/14/21; WSR 18-12-028, § 308-30-270, filed 5/29/18, effective 7/1/18.]

### 308-30-280 - Change of application information

If any of the information submitted on a notary public's commission or endorsement applications pursuant to WAC 308-30-030 changes, the notary public shall report this change to the department in writing within fifteen days.

[Statutory Authority: RCW 42.45.250. WSR 18-12-028, § 308-30-280, filed 5/29/18, effective 7/1/18.]

### 308-30-290 - Authorized remote notarial acts

(1) A notary public who has received both an electronic records notary public endorsement and a remote notarial acts endorsement from the department may perform the following remote notarial acts:

(a) Taking an acknowledgment;

(b) Taking a verification on oath or affirmation;

(c) Witnessing or attesting a signature;

(d) Certifying or attesting a copy;

(e) Certifying that an event has occurred or an act has been performed; and

(f) Noting a protest of a negotiable instrument, if the notary public is:

(i) Acting under the authority of an attorney who is licensed to practice law in this state or another state; or

(ii) Acting under the authority of a financial institution regulated by this state, another state, or the federal government.

(2) In performing remote notarial acts, a notary public shall comply with all requirements for electronic notarial acts under this chapter.

[Statutory Authority: RCW 42.45.250. WSR 21-05-039, § 308-30-290, filed 2/11/21, effective 3/14/21.]

### 308-30-300 - Standards for identity proofing

(1) In performing remote notarial acts, if a notary public does not have satisfactory evidence of the identity of a remotely located individual under subsection (4) of this section, the notary public must reasonably verify the individual's identity through two different types of identity proofing consisting of a credential analysis procedure and a dynamic knowledge-based authentication assessment as provided in subsections (2) and (3) of this section.

(2) Credential analysis must use public or private data sources to confirm the validity of the identification credential presented by a remotely located individual and shall, at a minimum:

(a) Use automated software processes to aid the notary public in verifying the identity of each remotely located individual;

(b) Require the identification credential to pass an authenticity test, consistent with sound commercial practices, that uses appropriate technologies to confirm the integrity of visual, physical, or cryptographic security features and to confirm that the identification credential is not fraudulent or inappropriately modified;

(c) Use information held or published by the issuing source or an authoritative source, as available and consistent with sound commercial practices, to confirm the validity of personal details and identification credential details; and

(d) Enable the notary public visually to compare for consistency the information and photograph on the identification credential and the remotely located individual as viewed by the notary public in real time through communication technology.

(3) A dynamic knowledge-based authentication assessment is successful if it meets the following requirements:

(a) The remotely located individual must answer a quiz consisting of a minimum of five questions related to the individual's personal history or identity formulated from public or private data sources;

(b) Each question must have a minimum of five possible answer choices;

(c) At least eighty percent of the questions must be answered correctly;

(d) All questions must be answered within two minutes;

(e) If the remotely located individual fails the first attempt, the individual may retake the quiz one time within twenty-four hours;

(f) During a retake of the quiz, a minimum of forty percent of the prior questions must be replaced;

(g) If the remotely located individual fails the second attempt, the individual is not allowed to retry with the same online notary public within twenty-four hours of the second failed attempt; and

(h) The notary public must not be able to see or record the questions or answers.

(4) A notary public has satisfactory evidence of the identity of a remotely located individual if:

(a) The notary public has personal knowledge of the identity of the individual; or

(b) The individual is identified by oath or affirmation of a credible witness in accordance with the following requirements:

(i) To be a credible witness, the witness must have personal knowledge of the remotely located individual;

(ii) The notary public must have personal knowledge of the credible witness or verify the identity of the credible witness by two different types of identity proofing in accordance with subsections (1), (2), and (3) of this section; and

(iii) A credible witness may be outside the physical presence of the notary public or remotely located individual if the notary public, credible witness, and remotely located individual can communicate by using communication technology.

[Statutory Authority: RCW 42.45.250. WSR 21-05-039, § 308-30-300, filed 2/11/21, effective 3/14/21.]

### 308-30-310 - Standards for communication technology

(1) Communication technology for remote notarial acts must provide for synchronous audio-visual feeds of sufficient audio clarity and video resolution to enable the notary public and remotely located individual to see and speak with each other. The process must provide a means for the notary public reasonably to confirm that an electronic record before the notary public is the same record in which the remotely located individual made a statement or on which the remotely located individual executed a signature.

(2) Communication technology must provide reasonable security measures to prevent unauthorized access to:

(a) The live transmission of the audio-visual feeds;

(b) The methods used to perform identify verification; and

(c) The electronic record that is the subject of the remote notarial act.

(3) If a remotely located individual must exit the workflow, the individual must restart the identify verification process required under WAC 308-30-300 from the beginning.

[Statutory Authority: RCW 42.45.250. WSR 21-05-039, § 308-30-310, filed 2/11/21, effective 3/14/21.]

### 308-30-320 - Certificate of notarial act for remote notarial acts

(1) A form of notarial certificate for a remote notarial act satisfies the requirement of RCW 42.45.280(4) and 42.45.130 (1)(g) if it is in the form provided by applicable law and contains a statement substantially as follows: "This notarial act involved the use of communication technology."

(2) A short form of acknowledgment prescribed in RCW 42.45.140 satisfies the requirement of RCW 42.45.280(4) and 42.45.130 (1)(g) if it is in substantially one of the following forms for the purposes indicated:

(a) For an acknowledgment in an individual capacity:

> State of Washington
> County of .......
>
> This record was acknowledged before me by means of communication technology on (date) by (name(s) of individuals).
>
> . . . .
> (Signature of notary public)
> Notary Public                     (Electronic official stamp)
> (My commission expires: . . . .)

(b) For an acknowledgment in a representative capacity:

> State of Washington
> County of .......
>
> This record was acknowledged before me by means of communication technology on (date) by (name(s) of individuals) as (type of authority, such as officer or trustee) of (name of party on behalf of whom the instrument was executed).
>
> . . . .
> (Signature of notary public)
> Notary Public                     (Electronic official stamp)
> (My commission expires: . . . .)

(c) For verification on oath or affirmation:

> State of Washington
> County of .......
>
> Signed and sworn to (or affirmed) before me by means of communication technology on (date) by (name(s) of individuals making statement).
>
> . . . .
> (Signature of notary public)
> Notary Public                     (Electronic official stamp)
> (My commission expires: . . . .)

(d) For witnessing or attesting a signature:

> State of Washington
> County of .......

Signed or attested before me by means of communication technology on (date) by (name(s) of individuals).

. . . .

(Signature of notary public)
Notary Public              (Electronic official stamp)
(My commission expires: . . . .)

[Statutory Authority: RCW 42.45.250. WSR 21-05-039, § 308-30-320, filed 2/11/21, effective 3/14/21.]

**308-30-330 - Retention of audio-visual recordings and repositories**

(1) A notary public must retain any audio-visual recording created under RCW 42.45.280 (3)(c) in a computer or other electronic storage device that protects the recording against unauthorized access by password or other secure means of authentication. The recording must be created in an industry-standard audio-visual file format and must not include images of any electronic record that was the subject of the remote notarial act.

(2) An audio-visual recording must be retained for at least ten years after the recording is made.

(3) A notary public must take reasonable steps to ensure that a backup of the audio-visual recording exists and is secure from unauthorized use.

(4) The fact that the notary public's employer, contractor, or repository keeps or stores any audio-visual recordings shall not relieve the notary of the duties required by these rules.

(5) The personal representative or guardian of a notary public shall follow RCW 42.45.280(6) related to the disposition of the notary public's audio-visual recordings upon the death or adjudication of incompetency of the notary public.

(6) The notary public, or the notary's personal representative or guardian, shall provide access instructions to the department for any audio-visual recordings maintained or stored by the notary, upon commission resignation, revocation, or expiration without renewal, or upon the death of adjudication of incompetency of the notary.

(7) A notary public, or the notary's personal representative or guardian, may by written contract engage a third party to act as a repository to provide the storage required by this section. A third party under contract under this section shall be deemed a repository under RCW 42.45.280(6).

(8) Any contract under subsection (7) of this section must:

(a) Enable the notary public, or the notary's personal representative or guardian, to comply with the retention requirements of this section even if the contract is terminated; or

(b) Provide that the information will be transferred to the notary public, or to the notary's personal representative or guardian, if the contract is terminated.

[Statutory Authority: RCW 42.45.250. WSR 21-05-039, § 308-30-330, filed 2/11/21, effective 3/14/21.] ■

# About the NNA

Since 1957, the National Notary Association has been committed to serving and educating the nation's Notaries. During that time, the NNA® has become known as the most trusted source of information for and about Notaries and Notary laws, rules and best practices.

The NNA serves Notaries through its NationalNotary.org website, social media, publications, annual conferences, seminars, online training and the NNA® Hotline, which offers immediate answers to specific questions about notarization.

In addition, the NNA offers the highest quality professional supplies, including official seals and stamps, recordkeeping journals, Notary certificates and Notary bonds.

Though dedicated primarily to educating and assisting Notaries, the NNA supports implementing effective Notary laws and informing the public about the Notary's vital role in today's society.

To learn more about the National Notary Association, visit NationalNotary.org. ∎

# Index

## A

Acknowledgments .......................... 23–25
Additional RON
 requirements ............................... 51–53
Address change ................................ 5–6
Affirmations .................................... 27–28
*Apostilles* ............................................. 18
Appeal of denial or revocation ....... 60
Application for commission .......... 3–4
Authentication ............................... 17–18
Authorized acts .............................. 22–23
Awareness ............................................. 8

## B

Becoming an electronic records or
 remote Notary Public ............. 48–49
Blank documents ............................... 14
Bond, Notary ..................................... 4–5

## C

Certificate forms ........................... 40–41
Certificate, Notary ........................ 39–42
Certification of an event or
 act ............................................... 30–31
Certified copies ............................. 25–26
Credible identifying
 witnesses ................................... 10–11

## D

Depositions ................................... 26–27
Disqualifying interest ....................... 15

## E

Electronic journal ........................ 50–51
Electronic notarization .............. 46–48
Electronic signature ................... 49–50
Electronic stamp ................................ 49
Errors and omissions insurance ....... 5

## F

Faxes .................................................... 14
Fees for Notary services ............ 33–34
Fines ................................................ 55–59
Foreign languages ............................. 18

## H

*Hague Convention Abolishing the
 Requirement of Legalization for
 Foreign Public Documents* ........... 18

## I

Identification documents (ID
 cards) ........................................... 9–10
Identifying document signers ...... 8–9
Illegal and improper acts .......... 58–60

Immigration Services Fraud
Prevention Act ................18–20
Incomplete documents .................14
In-person electronic
 notarization .....................46–52
In-person electronic notarizations
 and remote online notarizations
 defined ..............................46–48

**J**

Journal of notarial acts ............... 35–38
Jurisdiction .................................5

**L**

Locus sigilli (L.S.) ......................44

**M**

Minors, notarizing for ...............13–14
Misconduct .............................55–59

**N**

Name change ............................. 6

**O**

Oaths ..................................27–28

**P**

Penalties ..............................55–59
Personal appearance .......................7
Personal knowledge of identity ...... 9
Photocopies ...............................14
Protests ..............................31–33

**R**

Reasonable care ........................16
Refusal of services ................. 15–16
Relatives ..................................15
Remote online notarization ...... 46–52
Representative capacity ............... 24
Resignation ...........................5–6
Restriction of commission ....... 55–58
Revocation .............................. 58

**S**

Satisfactory evidence of identity ... 9
Signature by mark ..................11–12
Signature by proxy ..................12–13
Stamp, Notary ....................... 43–45

**T**

Term of office ..............................5

**U**

Unauthorized acts ....................... 34
Unauthorized practice of law ... 16–17

**V**

Verifications upon oath or
 affirmation ...................... 28–29

**W**

Willingness ...............................7
Wills .....................................21
Witnessing or attesting a
 signature .........................29–30

Index | 97

**Notes**

# Notes

## Notes

## Notes

## Notes

# Notes

# Notes